Narrative
Suspense

Narrative Suspense

"When Slim
Turned Sideways . . ."

Eric S. Rabkin

Ann Arbor
The University of Michigan Press

PN
218
R3

Acknowledgments are extended to the following publishers and authors for
permission to reprint copyright materials.

American Folklore Society, Inc., for excerpts from Vladimir Propp, "The
Swan-Geese," from *Morphology of the Folktale*, 2nd edition, translated
by Laurence Scott.

American Psychological Association and Roger Brown, for an excerpt from
Roger Brown, "How Shall a Thing Be Called," *Psychological Review*,
vol. 65, 1958. Copyright 1958 by the American Psychological Association.

Grossman Publishers, for an excerpt from Gaston Bachelard, *The Poetics
of Space*, translated by Maria Jolas. Translation Copyright © 1964 by
The Orion Press. Reprinted by permission of Grossman Publishers.

Holt, Rinehart and Winston, Inc., for a brief excerpt from Anon., *Lazarillo
de Tormes*, translated by Mack Hendricks Singleton, from *Masterpieces
of the Spanish Golden Age*, edited by Angel Flores.

Johnson Reprint Corporation, for material from A. R. Luria, "The Directive Function of Speech in Development and Dissolution, Part I" as
reprinted in *Language*, edited by R. C. Oldfield and J. C. Marshall.

Alfred A. Knopf, Inc., for excerpts from Thomas Mann, *Death in Venice
and Seven Other Stories*.

Tom Lehrer, for lyrics to "Oedipus Rex" from *More of Tom Lehrer*, © 1959
by Tom Lehrer. Used by permission.

Penguin Books Ltd., for short excerpts from Gottfried von Strassburg,
Tristan, translated by A. T. Hatto. Copyright©1960 by A. T. Hatto. And
for excerpts from Longus, *Daphnis and Chloe*, translated by Paul
Turner, Copyright © 1968 by Paul Turner.

University of Nebraska Press, for material from George Bird Grinnell,
"The Ghost Wife," from *Pawnee Hero Stories and Folk-Tales;* and for
Anon., "Howleglass," from *A Hundred Merry Tales*, edited by P. M.
Zall.

For Betty

Consider the death of a queen. If it is in a story we say "and then?"

—E. M. FORSTER, *Aspects of the Novel*

Preface

The enterprise of this book is to bring readers and critics closer together. As critics, we discuss works which we have read, analyzing the relations of the parts to the whole. As readers, we concern ourselves with what has come before and what will be read, waiting to see how the next bit of text will compare with that which has preceded it. When the bit of text is a bit of plot, and when we are conscious of the waiting, we call the force that draws us through a narrative suspense. But we know that we can be drawn through a narrative by its style, say, or the development of its theme. I should like to call the momentary engagement with these temporal structures, as well as the structures of plot, suspense. Such a conception of suspense obviously diverges from traditional usage. I hope this book will demonstrate the utility for so radical a generalization of a familiar notion.

Contents

Introduction

We all like to read books. Even among teachers and critics, it is likely that the pleasures of reading a book surpass those of discussing it. And yet most of the discussions of literature we encounter focus not on this activity of reading, but on the "motionless memory"[1] that we are left with after the reading is done. In fact, people who like to talk about books, myself included, don't often care which book they're talking about: again, what is attractive is the activity, not the object.

T. S. Eliot[2] said that although we judge the literariness of books by literary standards, we must add extraliterary standards to our discussion of a book's greatness. Edward Taylor (d. 1729) strikes me as a good poet. I come back again and again to lines like, "Who in this Bowling Alley Bowld the Sun?"[3] There is something in the way the line rolls that makes the image come alive for me; each time I read "Who in this Bowling Alley Bowld the Sun?" I see the hand of God sweeping across the blue skies of man's best firmament. But I am quick to admit that using Eliot's analysis Taylor is not a great poet. How could he be? With the exception of a few friends who read only a handful of his poems in manuscript, Taylor the poet made no impact on the world at all until Thomas H. Johnson fortunately found and published a broad sampling of his poems in 1939, over two hundred years after their composition. *Uncle Tom's Cabin,* on the other hand, is not, as literature, high on the list of American productions. There are few readers today who would compare its artistic merits with those of the works of Melville, Hawthorne, James, or Hemingway. In fact, few would even compare Mrs. Stowe's literary accomplishments with the currently disfavored abilities of Cooper or Poe. And yet certainly *Uncle Tom's Cabin* is, in its way, one of the greatest books of the modern age. Its immediate impact and wide distribution are rivaled by only a few books: *The Sorrows of Young Werther* which sparked a wave of suicides across the Continent; Rousseau's *Confessions* which in one stroke apparently changed our fictional possibilities; Tom Paine's *Common Sense* which roused a whole class of Americans to the then-current cause of revolution; Mao's *Thoughts* which (reportedly) cure appendicitis. But at this point we have again turned from the activity of reading and elevated its object.

At a certain moment we are ripe to read a certain book, our *interest* in it pre-exists and we are attracted almost purely by its content. For example, *Portnoy's Complaint* by Philip Roth (which I happen to think is also a good book) achieved at least temporary greatness. The current interest in "artistic freedom" to discuss "forbidden" subjects prompts enormous sales. The need then to have read the book, to have made it part of one's mental possessions, arises as a social exigency: no one dares go to a cocktail party unarmed. But such interest does not make a book literarily good. *Sex Sorceress*[4] and its legion brethren, the self-advertised pornography with the big print and the "full-color" illustrations, are achieving equally impressive distribution. Our courts are allowing it and suddenly (fortunately) even people without college degrees have the right to read erotic literature. Today, the whole genre is sociologically great. But only some books of that genre are literarily good.

Such a distinction between greatness and goodness, between the literary object and the reading activity, is not at all new. This is the phenomenon we encounter in nineteenth-century England with maidens wasting their youths (if one may believe the antiliterarians) weeping over romantic novel after romantic novel. The girls knew what to expect when they picked one up: there were conventions of titling, binding, and format; there were favored authors; there was word of mouth. The same is true of today's erotic literature. I would guess that Roth's work will be adjudged good; I know that George Eliot's has been. But clearly the reasons behind this judgment, as T. S. Eliot implies, are not reasons of private, static, historically or sociologically motivated interest.

In one sense, interest can be very narrow. I knew a boy in high school who would read anything that promised to be about trains; and he would read nothing else. There was no use telling him Rousseau's *Confessions* is a great book, or that it is a good book. When there is no interest, books will not get read.

In another sense, however, interest can be very broad. One might be tempted to say that someone is interested simply in reading good books. I, for one, am. However, when we expand the concept of interest to that extent, it no longer serves to indicate possible *loci* for one's engagement with a text. After all, then, by definition, one reads a book because one is merely interested; fails to read it because one is not. We have ignored compulsion, that driving attraction that good books all seem to work on us.

To the extent that a form/content distinction is useful, interest can usefully be taken to indicate a reader's engagement with content. Through sociology of knowledge[5] we may be able to study interest for particular groups (say the popularity of Cameron Hawley's business novels among the lower middle class of America in the 1950s) or, through psychoanalysis, we may be able to study interest for individuals (say Baudelaire's famous affinity for Poe). But these interests come from outside the work. The reader must supply them.

Within the work, however, we find all manner of things: metaphors and morals, plots and people, themes and therapy. Of course, where there is no interest these things become inaccessible. Who wouldn't put down a book, no matter how highly touted, were one to recognize in the first pages that a successful reading depended upon one's genuinely liking that which one genuinely hates? But such occurrences are rare. For most of us who like reading, whatever the state of our positive interests, our negative interests are not frequently strong enough to make a difference. At least, this is my case.

With Empson, I plead an inability to discuss well a work that I do not like. If I like it, it could not assault my interests too strongly. In fact, knowing about the eternal verities and the exalted value of art, I might even guess that if I like it, it appeals to my interests at least in some small way. Being thus "willing"[6] to read, I have access to that strange collection of things that books present us.

Two observations need be adduced to get us to the other side of the form/content distinction: (1) specific interests from general interests grow; (2)

4

books are made of language and pages. Consider Melville's *Typee* (publ. 1846) against the American audience of its day. Those were the times of Manifest Destiny. America resided between, and presided over, the earth's two greatest oceans. Our industries were burgeoning, our commerce seeking foreign markets, our navy expanding. There was a general interest in the sea and in exploration. A reader of that decade needed only to read Melville's title page:[7]

TYPEE:

A Peep at Polynesian Life

During a

Four Months' Residence

in

A Valley of the Marquesas

and presto! The reader with a general interest in the literature of sea and exploration develops a specific interest in this strange and far-off island group. But, when our expectant reader begins, he finds himself not on an island, but on a ship. The Marquesas, as the annotated table of contents would tell him, are still one chapter south-by-southwest. Well, he doesn't really know what he's missing anyway: he's never read about the Marquesas before. And reading about being on a ship is a good way to spend the waiting time. The process might even (it does in Melville) put what follows into context. And so our reader is into the progression of the things that are in the book. He is not in this progression though as McLuhan[8] asserts, because the language is written from left to right, top to bottom. Of course, our written language is linear. And of course, then, it must present progressions. But he is into this progression because, having been interested by the title, he waits now to find out more. "And then?" He waits. And he reads while he waits. This is suspense—and the subject of this study.

I
Subliminal Knowledge

The Foundation For Suspense

Subliminal Knowledge

"We can know more than we can tell."[1] Who would fail to recognize a good friend after a year's absence? And yet, who can say in advance whether that friend's eyebrows meet at the bridge of the nose, or whether the corners of the mouth are pinched by smile lines, or whether the hair is parted on the right or left? Of course, some one or other of these things we might know to tell, but not the others. Gombrich[2] has shown through the easy recognition of caricatures and cartoons that certain key features are all that one requires for instant identification. And yet, as Gombrich himself points out, given the actual face, not some reproduction (like a cartoon), a discrepancy in any of the inessential features is often enough to prevent recognition. In any given situation, there is some knowledge more unconscious than the knowledge of which we are aware.

For example, it may be the case that you are thinking about what you are reading at this moment. If you are, then it is impossible that you are thinking about how to read these words. That you must know "tacitly,"[3] as Polanyi says. I would call such knowledge subliminal—it operates below one's level of conscious perception. Your response to the ideas on these pages is tempered by your agreement, bewilderment, boredom; your response to the practice of reading is unthinking. We depend upon knowledge of particulars to apprehend wholes. This is true not merely of reading, but also of learning a foreign language, driving a car, recognizing a friend, anything that involves man's epistemologic capabilities. On this base rest the edifices of phenomenology, gestalt psychology, and physical education. We assume subliminal knowledge of particulars in order to consciously grasp wholes. When the salesman asks, "In red or blue?" one rarely has the presence of mind to respond, "Neither."

The easiest way to appreciate the potency of subliminal knowledge is to remember the first time when, driving a car, it began to snow. You told yourself that if you should hit a slick spot, turn *into* the skid, not away. Into it, not away. A simple thought, but one that you knew would be hard to keep in mind because it is so "natural" to try to recover the road. And besides, the driver's manual told you that your first reaction would be the wrong one. And then that sick feeling, the wheels sliding out, you spin the wheel, right, left, recover, foot off accelerator, no braking, turn back the smallest bit, recover traction, slight acceleration, and ease back onto the road. All in a breath. And all done like a professional.

It is possible that part of these complicated maneuvers were motivated consciously. But did you direct your foot off the accelerator? No. Your unconscious knowledge saved your life, and does so every day. It is our confidence in our subliminal knowledge of particulars that gives us the faith to drive a car, touch type, or climb a flight of stairs (even with closed eyes!). But it is only in moments of crisis that we are made jarringly aware of the wealth of unconscious knowledge, subliminal knowledge, that we carry with us, knowledge almost as close to us as our sense of our names and identity. In the quiet moments, when we drive with the radio on, we assume this subliminal knowledge which nonetheless influences all the more conscious knowledge of that moment. When we are distracted by thoughts, great ideas, the imagery of a poem, we assume our knowledge of syntax and reading motor skills and security in the armchair. It is just because this knowledge is taken for granted and operates below the level of our consciousness that its impact is so strong.

One should not, however, conclude from the nature of these illustrations that subliminal knowledge is an aspect of lower-level thinking alone, motor skills and such. Consider the following gem from Will Rogers's *Illiterate Digest:*[4]

Two Lost Friends Found at Last

Well, sir, I have a real Message for my readers. It looked like it would be just the ordinary Article with no flavor or Backbone or Truth, and with no real underlying news or wisdom, that is, nothing that the people would be glad to know and read. As I say, that is the kind of Article I thought it would be. But as I picked up the morning papers, why, I read who was in our midst out here in Sunny California. Well, sir, it struck me like a thunderbolt here was news which my public had been longing for for years and here I had found it out!

Well, I says to myself, this is too good to keep, for here people had been wondering all this time for just what I knew now. I kinder hated to leave the East on account of thinking I would be out of touch

with some of our National Characters but I find
that sooner or later they all arrive out here and
start in fighting off Real Estate men the same as
shooing away Mosquitoes on Long Island.

Well, who should blow in but two of our old long-
lost friends, and I know that even 'Frisco (who is
jealous of any one being here) will be glad to hear
they are here well and hearty, and rehearsed their
old Act here yesterday and people enjoyed them just
as much as they did in the old days.

Both of these Boys were on the big time and were
well known all around the Circuit, and any time
they took the Platform standing by the side of a
Pitcher of ice water and a glass, why, it just meant
6 columns starting on the front page and ending
among the want ads. I bet you hadn't heard of them
in years and will thank me for resurrecting this information for you.

I can't keep it any longer. I did want to keep it till
the finish of this to tell you but I must tell you now
who they are—William J. Bryan and Billy Sunday!

Mr. Rogers certainly has not much of a punch
line for an audience of our decade. But still we,
readers and critics alike, can sense that the engagement with this piece is through suspense. From the title, "Two Lost Friends Found at Last," to the last
sentence whose very syntax is strung out, holding the
answer at bay, we are kept asking, "Who?" In some
complex way, this is equivalent to the question
Forster raises for plot: "And then?" We have some interest, aroused perhaps from the title, perhaps from
the first exposure to an unusual style, perhaps from
the odd habits of capitalization, and that interest
gives us access to a structure, a question to be
answered, and reminds us time and again that we
are not done (something like tonality in music) until
we have the answer to the question, "Who?"

Surpringly, the disappointing answer, for me at least, is in itself a reason to go on. Why, I wonder, is Rogers so concerned about these two? Is it a function of the time at which he is writing? Is it the unusual conjunction of fields of endeavor? Is the interest on the author's part perhaps feigned?[5]

Regardless of the answer to these questions, a reader, even one not formally educated in criticism, has access in a conscious way to techniques that created the suspense. We all recognize a promise-to-be-fulfilled in the first paragraph; we see how, by using phrases like "too good to keep" and epithets like "National Characters" the weight of the promised result is intensified in the second paragraph; we see that "their old Act" in the third paragraph is intentionally ambiguous, intentionally suspenseful; and, with references to newspapers and such, we easily see how the fourth paragraph again intensifies our anticipation. We have conscious access to these bits of conscious knowledge. Let us call the suspense they create *conscious suspense*. But we also must have subliminal knowledge of the passage. How does that function?

I. A. Richards[6] writes:

> Whenever we hear or read any not too nonsensical opinion, a tendency so strong and so automatic that it must have been formed along with our earliest speech habits, leads us to consider *what seems to be said* rather than the *mental operations* of the persons who said it. If the speaker is a recognized and obvious liar this tendency is, of course, arrested. We do then neglect what he has said and turn our attention instead to the motives or mechanisms that have caused him to say it. [Emphasis his.]

The power of this insight, I think, and the ability to

Narrative Suspense

generalize it, depend upon making a distinction that
Richards himself raises:

> I shall keep the term *"statement"* for those
> utterances whose "meaning" in the sense of what
> they say, or purport to say, is the prime object of in-
> terest. I shall reserve the term *"expression"* for
> those utterances where it is the mental operations
> of the writers which are to be considered.
> [Emphasis mine.][7]

In other words, we have conscious knowledge of statement alone unless we sense that the writer is not being
straightforward; in that case our knowledge of expression, which would normally be subliminal, suddenly
becomes conscious. When this happens with a good
writer, we are being asked to appreciate him for his artifice. Allow me to repeat part of Rogers's column and
continue it:

> Well, who should blow in but two of our old long-
> lost friends, and I know that even 'Frisco (who is
> jealous of any one being here) will be glad to hear
> they are here well and hearty, and rehearsed their
> old Act here yesterday and people enjoyed them just
> as much as they did in the old days.
>
> Both of these Boys were on the big time and were
> well known all around the Circuit, and any time
> they took the Platform standing by the side of a
> Pitcher of ice water and a glass, why, it just meant
> 6 columns starting on the front page and ending
> among the want ads. I bet you hadn't heard of them
> in years and will thank me for resurrecting this in-
> formation for you.
>
> I can't keep it any longer. I did want to keep it till
> the finish of this [obviously still eight pages away
> to anyone holding the book—ESR] to tell you but I
> must tell you now who they are—William J. Bryan
> and Billy Sunday!
>
> Neither did I, but *they are,* and looking fine.

Now that is artifice! We all know the missing line: "I didn't know that *they* were still alive!" The fact that we know it, and all know in about the same way, should make us suddenly aware that Rogers was doing much more to us than we were at first conscious of. Here something is obviously left out. Here a subliminal structure is violated. Now that our concern is so dramatically shifted to the expression rather than the statement of the passage, we realize the weight of "old long-lost," "well and hearty," "rehearsed," "yesterday," "in the old days," "in years," and, almost paradigmatically, "resurrecting." Suddenly the previously disappointing answer, Bryan and Billy Sunday, fades into insignificance. With a shock made possible by the heightening of suspense, we have ourselves completed a subliminal structure, based on subliminal knowledge. That such knowledge was not apparent until after we had encountered the last quoted line indicates its subliminal nature.[8] That the artistry of the lengthier passage seems so much more satisfying, I believe, indicates how much more fundamental to our experience of the text is our subliminal knowledge than our conscious knowledge.

A good lie, as Oscar Wilde said, "is that which contains its own truth."[9] Through Rogers's tall tales, advertised by their statement as false, Rogers was able to construct subliminal structures that supported some of the best social and political criticism ever spun in this country. The whole of *Illiterate Digest* is worth reading even though the issues themselves are now past. What must be noted here is that such a notion of liar, a notion which can include Will Rogers, generalizes Richards's idea to the point that we may say that whenever something is not stated so as to be necessarily believable, we change our conscious focus of interest to its manner of expression. The effects of

13

expression are more potent than the effects of statement. And the on-again-off-again consciousness of expression, the shift in our progression through the text of our subliminal awareness up and down through consciousness, provides the aesthetic pleasure of reading even such texts as are concerned with dead issues. To say that expression is essential to narrative is to underscore the fundamental importance of rhetoric.

Metaphor and Irony

Metaphors are usually looked upon as objects rather than activities; their impact is considered to be synchronic, static, patterned, rather than diachronic, active, rhythmic. Most critics conceive of metaphors out of time, as they conceive of books themselves out of time. And these same critics[10] find that all rhetoric is based upon metaphor: the connection between narrative and style is radical.

I agree fully with this conclusion: the surface of the work, the style, the language, is its most engaging and pervasive aspect. However, I hold this for quite different reasons. This connection exists not because both narratives and metaphors are objects, but because both are activities. That is, I admit that after reading a novel, that novel may take on a permanent shape in the files of our minds. I also admit that our "memory" of metaphors is motionless. But we all know from the first page of most books, and at each point in time in the reading, whether or not the book is good; and the goodness of metaphors too comes from the activity of the reading, the surprise of the closing of the figure. We can say that all rhetorical devices associate something in some way with something, and so reduce all rhetoric to figural metaphor (as Burke does),[11] but this has three pernicious effects: (1) this two-part notion of metaphor conceals the role of context in determining meaning and effect; (2) an extreme reduction obscures the strong family relation between metaphor and irony; (3) the figural notion implies that our responses to metaphor are to *faits accomplis* rather than to experiences, that our engagement with metaphor is synchronic rather than diachronic, of interest rather than of suspense.

Consider the sentence, "He is a lion!" Is it a metaphor? No, not if the speaker is referring to a lion; yes, if he is referring to a brave man; neither, if he is referring to a coward. (This last alternative is clearly irony.) Let us assume the context in which "He is a lion!" is a metaphor. Normally, one would say that *He* is the tenor of the metaphor and *lion* is the vehicle.[12] This terminology, however, is applicable only to metaphors that conveniently present us with two separable parts. Most metaphors are actually single words operating within a context. Verbs, for instance, often serve as metaphors favored by writers for their potential vividness.

> **The editor stopped turning over his manuscript. "Let's see," he said, holding out his hand for Bartley's article. He looked at the first headline, "What I Know about Logging," and smiled. "Old, but good." Then he glanced at the other headings, and ran his eye down the long strips on which Bartley had written; nibbled at the text here and there a little . . .[13]**

Nibbled, in this passage, is clearly metaphoric. But it is, apparently, both vehicle and tenor of the metaphor. Such an occurrence, in the context of the two-part theory of metaphor, is impossible. In fact, the theory errs in asserting that *he* and *lion* are related as two parts of a figure. *He* reactivates in our minds, at a subliminal level, its antecedent (say, brave man) which serves as a context. *Lion* is then compared with the implications of the context. We redefine one of the semantic features of *lion*, making a [−human] word [+human]. Now, this discrepancy by-passed, we see that all the other, unredefined features of *lion* (bravery, strength, courage, hairiness)[14] support the context. This procontextual (see Glossary, s.v. "Contextuality") comparison is metaphor. Similarly, in Howells, clearly the context concerns eyes, reading, intellection. *Nibbled* must be redefined, say (using arbitrary and nonstandard features now) [+mouth] to [−mouth] and [−eyes] to [+eyes]. The *un*redefined features support the context. Notice how tentatively the action is reported, how piecemeal; "strips"; "here and there a little." Nibbled is, in this context, a metaphor.

We can reverse the effect, produce an anticontextual (see Glossary, s.v. "Contextuality") comparison, by choosing a word which has reversed semantic features. Such a method quickly reveals how heavily writers depend on metaphoric comparisons, even when such comparisons are not obviously tropes. In order to minimize context, I've chosen a deceptively simple first line from a children's book:

> **It began on a villainously cold and sleety and tempest-twisted night in mid-December, one of those nights nobody wants.**[15]

The personification of the night in *villainously* is clearly metaphoric; after the necessary redefinition to make a [+Animate] word [−Animate], the unredefined features support the evil, tempestuous context, that is, they make a procontextual comparison with it. *Nobody wants* is also procontextual, calling for a strange type of redefinition which we might think of as cathexis; there is no standard term for this type of metaphor. But *nobody wants* is certainly not straightforward; it does function rhetorically, as we can see if we tamper with the semantic features.

It began on a villainously cold and sleety and tempest-twisted night in mid-December, one of those nights everybody wants.

Suddenly, by reversing the signs of the features which are *not* redefined, we find we have an example not of metaphor, but of irony. We can call any meaningful unit, as computer technicians do, a bit. The word *nobody* is a bit: it has reference on its own, but in a narrative it takes on meaning in context. Instead of reversing the features of this bit, let us reverse the features of the context.

It began on a benevolently warm and misty and zephyr-blown night in mid-June, one of those nights nobody wants.

Again, because of the anticontextual comparison that we make as we perceive *nobody,* we have irony. At this point, one could easily predict the result of reversing the features of both the context and the bit we perceive as compared with it.

It began on a benevolently warm and misty and zephyr-blown night in mid-June, one of those nights everybody wants.

Of course, we have metaphor again, just as in the first sentence. What these four versions reveal is that our responses to irony and our responses to metaphor are located in the same mechanisms; it is a yes-no situation, a matter of pro- and anticontextual comparisons. And we see the overwhelming importance of context, an analysis that obviates the need for the

17

terms *vehicle* and *tenor*.[16] And, in the balanced sentences of these descriptions, we see metaphor and irony arising through a temporal process.

Let us go back to our first metaphor. "He is a _____." One waits to have this completed. If we intend to read, then we must tacitly, subliminally, accept our own knowledge of syntax. We wait to find out what "he is." If, in the context of a brave man, we find out that he is a lion, we are aware of rhetoric because we must perform a mental redefinition. And, when the unredefined features are procontextual, we call this a metaphor. In the context of a coward, the assertion that he is a lion would similarly remind us that we are experiencing rhetoric, though with opposite effect, irony. However, only when a device such as not finishing the sentence interferes with our reading in the same way that the redefinition interferes with it are we aware that, even in the context of a real lion, "He is a lion!" depends upon the engagement of suspense. Syntax implies a temporal imperative, and to fail to accept this imperative is to lose the ability to read. To ignore syntax subliminally is to reduce language to an incoherent stream of noises. Of course we are not aware of the subliminal suspense built into our process notion of syntax when we read of a real lion that "he is a lion." Instead, we assume we have a propositional statement. To distinguish our reactions to this from our reactions to metaphor and irony, we could say that the comparison is neutral, rather than pro- or anticontextual. We must realize, though, that neutral comparisons are still comparisons of perceived bits with the context in which they occur, and our unconscious waiting for the perceived bit which will make the comparison is subliminal suspense, the same engagement with structure that motivates us in the question-answer structure of the Will Rogers passage, the same notion of looking forward for formal completion that informs all aspects of our reading.[17] To say this is to say that what we took to be the primacy of rhetoric (expression) (p. 14) is in fact the primacy of temporal structure, of subliminal suspense. It is this suspense that gives life to style.

For the sake of clarity, Terhune's opening line served nicely. For completeness, we should notice just how pervasively style depends upon our waiting for these comparisons. Please read the following slowly, bearing in mind the relationship of "vivid" words to metaphor:

> **They walked to the edge of the porch. The moistures of May** *drowned* **all save the most** *ardent* **stars, and gave back to the earth the** *sublimated* **light of the** *prostrate* **city.** *Deep in* **the end of the back yard, the blossoming peach tree** *shone* **like a** *celestial sentinel.* **The** *fecund* **air** *lavished* **upon their faces the tenderness of lovers'** *adoring* **hands, the dissolving fragrance of the** *opened* **world, which** *slept* **against the sky. [Emphasis mine.]**[18]

The italicized words are undoubtedly metaphoric. But the metaphoric structure of the style is even more complex than their frequency indicates. "Air" cannot "lavish" anything, much less "tenderness"; nor can "hands" "adore." Yet Agee's "air lavished . . . the tenderness of lovers' adoring hands." We have metaphor within metaphor; that is to say, structures are begun, and their completion is suspended while other structures are begun, and the subliminal suspense that keeps us going until the comparison is made is multiplied by the device. This creates an extraordinarily strong engagement with style.

Passages which show anticontextual comparisons are actually easier to find in modern literature than the procontextual type above. This is a function, I think, of our world-view: reality is capricious, inconsistent, harsh. The stylistic corollary of this view is irony, the anticontextual impinging on its context.

> **Yossarian could run into the hospital whenever he wanted to because of his liver and because of his eyes; the doctors couldn't fix his liver condition and couldn't meet his eyes each time he told them he had a liver condition.**[19]

This passage from *Catch-22* is typical of today's writing. It depends upon an absurdity (reflected in the style) that runs through such writers as Barthelme, Borges, Kosinski, and Vonnegut. This passage is also interesting in the way it employs parallelism. Were the parallelism of liver and eyes established before the semicolon carried out, then, after "couldn't fix his liver condition" we would expect something like "couldn't fix his eyes." The actual line is quite the opposite, reversing the expected semantic features, and creating an anticontextual comparison. The irony in this case then is neither semantic nor grammatical, but operates at some syntactic level in between. In fact, any temporal structure at any level of meaning can create the subliminal suspense that pulls us through a narrative.

In nineteenth-century American literature, one of the most striking devices that we find is actually the very same trick we used to explore the relationship between irony and metaphor: recontextualizing.[20] The following is from *Moby Dick*:[21]

> **Let me only say that it fared with him [Bulkington] as with the storm-tossed ship, that miserably drives along the lee-ward land [metaphor]. The port would fain give succor [metaphor]; the port is pitiful [antithetical metaphor]; in the port is safety,**

comfort, hearth-stone, supper, warm blankets, friends, all that's kind to our mortalities [procontextual use of first metaphor]. But in that gale, the port, the land, is that ship's direst jeopardy; she must fly all hospitality; one touch of land, though it but graze the keel, would make her shudder through and through [procontextual use of second metaphor]. With all her might she crowds all sail off shore; in so doing, fights, 'gainst the very winds that fain would blow her homeward; seeks all the lashed sea's landlessness again; for refuge's sake forlornly rushing into peril; her only friend her bitterest foe [alternating procontextual metaphors by isocolons, ending in an oxymoron].

This passage is drawn from the chapter titled simply, "The Lee Shore." By recontextualizing, Melville keeps always within the procontextual bounds of metaphor. However, as a by-product, he establishes a double context (for which a metaphoric expression is the final oxymoron). Thus he builds of the lee shore a vital symbol. In the same strictly metaphoric way, he presents the doubloon later in the book. In the same strictly metaphoric way, Hawthorne gives us the final multiplex symbol of the scarlet A. In the same strictly metaphoric way, Poe creates the cask of Amontillado.[22]

The prevalence of this technique characterizes a time and a place. Of more general applicability is the notion that all symbols take on meaning by functioning in context after context. This is just as true of anticontextual comparisons as it is of procontextual ones, of irony as of metaphor.

"This a good place," he [Cohn] said.
"There's a lot of liquor," I agreed.[23]

The force of *agreed* is to define *good* for the second speaker. It establishes a context, and in this context lie the structures of the narrative that keep us reading on. At any point in reading, our responses to a perceived bit depend upon all that we have been waiting for, all that has come before, context.

Context

Context (for the perceived bit) is the perceptual freight that we readers must carry forward with us in order to understand the significance of a bit as we perceive it. Such a definition loads a great deal on a relatively simple concept and implies a startling and various utility. As McLuhan tells us, we cannot even read an account of, say, a crime, without considering whether the context is that of the novel or the newspaper, a context established by the simplest physical means: we know *An American Tragedy*[24] is different from an article in *The New York Times* even before we start reading; the interest in *Compulsion* and *In Cold Blood* is largely a function of the intentional confusion between their journalistic content and literary form. More importantly, within a work of literature, our overt encounters with unavoidable problems of context are everywhere: the interpolated stories of *Don Quixote,* the treatise on time within Melville's *Pierre,* the Grand Inquisitor section of *The Brothers Karamazov,* the monograph on personality in Hesse's *Steppenwolf,* the personal letters in *Miss Lonelyhearts,* the central myth chapter in *House of the Seven Gables,* the stories characters tell each other in *Metamorphoses* on the one hand or in the tales of Isak Dinesen on the other—all these make us ask why? why does *this* appear *here?* and just *now?* what does this mean for the characters? for the story? Not surprisingly, these questions pose problems that we learn to solve long before we begin any formal

training in literature—we all know the possible
significance of the riddle posed to the hero two pages
into a fairy story, or two paragraphs into Oedipus.
When Richards spoke of an "obvious liar" (p.
11), the truth of his assertion rested not on the moral
situation, but on the simple observation we all make
that, when someone lies, he has his own purposes. So
much must also be said of a narrator. When a narrator
is "obvious," we question him in the same way that
we question a liar: we do not ask so much what he
says, but why he says it. Why is it important to our
understanding of Alyosha (to say nothing of Ivan,
Mitya, and the book) that we read the parable of the
Grand Inquisitor? What is important here is the
observation that answering this question about
Alyosha is much easier than answering the question:
"What is the meaning of the parable of the Grand
Inquisitor?" One would expect the reverse, since an
answer to the latter question is apparently necessary
to the answering of the former, but in fact this is not
so. Jesus' parables are subject to everlasting exegesis
by virtue of their spare context. A good parable has
countless meanings, times when it applies brilliantly
to the situation. As we read *The Brothers Karamazov,*
we do not catalog the possible meanings of
Dostoevski's parable; we leap immediately toward
relevant significance. This is precisely equivalent to
the experimental "finding that the intelligibility of a
sentence increases in the presence of a correct description of its general topic."[25] At the instant that we
finish reading the parable, its signification is
perceived as a bit which compares with the total context of Alyosha's developing (recontextualizing)
character, and, in this case, most immediately reinforces our notions about the futility of the young
man's piety. This comparison is procontextual then,

23

and in a real sense the parable acts metaphorically in relation to the whole book.

Like metaphor considered stylistically, such a comparison depends for its vigor on suspense, on the temporal separation of the context from the perceived bit. The greater the separation, the more overwhelmingly is the context important in directing our response. (This, of course, is true only insofar as, during the reading of the perceived bit, we at least subliminally recognize its relevant context. In the case of Dostoevski, the clear separation of Alyosha from his brothers, the environment of the monastery, and the strength of the influence of Father Zossima have already taught us that, while reading *The Brothers Karamazov,* religious references operate within a context that includes Alyosha.) The experimental evidence for the importance of context is overwhelming; certainly one example is worth citing:

> Let us . . . establish how effective the orienting (attention-directing) and directive role of a visual signal and its trace can be at this stage. We place before a child two inverted objects, a cup and a tumbler of non-transparent plastic. As the child watches, we hide a coin under the cup, which is placed to the left, and we ask the child to 'find' it. For a child of 1;4 to 1;6 [one year four months to one year six months], this constitutes an interesting and meaningful task, which he solves without difficulty. We repeat this experiment three or four times, each time holding the coin under the cup within sight of the child. The solution will invariably be successful. Now, without interrupting the experiment, we change its conditions and hide the coin not under the cup on the left, but under the tumbler on the right. A certain proportion of

children of the younger group will follow not the changed visual signal (more precisely, its trace), but the *influence of the inert motor stereotype,* and will put out their hands toward the cup on the left, carrying out the habitual movement reinforced in the previous experiment; only then will they turn to the tumbler under which the coin is hidden.

Let us now weaken the influence of the visual signal. We repeat the first experiment, but impose a short, ten-second delay between the hiding of the coin under the cup and the execution of the movement. This forces the child to act according to the *traces* of the visual signal whose effectiveness we are considering. The majority of children in the younger group successfully execute this task; only a few, the very youngest, cease to subordinate their actions to the visual instruction and begin to grasp both objects, losing track of finding the coin that is hidden under one of them.

However, we again modify the conditions and after repeating the experiment three or four times with the cup and the ten-second delay we hide the coin under the tumbler located on the right, all within sight of the child. The picture now changes substantially. The ten-second delay turns out to be sufficient for the visual signal to yield its place to the decisive influence of the reinforced motor habit. The overwhelming majority of children now repeat the movement directed toward the cup on the left, ceasing to be directed by the image of the coin hidden under the tumbler on the right.[26]

In this experiment, the context established by earlier learning becomes more and more important in accomplishing the total task as the time between the learning and the accomplishment grows, regardless of the intervening presence of a new signal. In our example from Dostoevski, the possible significations of the parable become unimportant after, under the in-

25

fluence of the learned context, we have chosen particular significations to integrate into our progressive reading of the whole work. We still operate within the structure that forces inquiries about the development of the characters of the novel, but cease to be concerned with the characters of the parable. The practice of writers shows an awareness of the overriding power of context and its functioning through time.

Although we can in some sense forget the central parable and go on with the story of the brothers because the context is so much more massive than the perceived bit, we cannot suffer similar lapses when the bit is actually more voluminous than the context. Such is the case in a very common form, the framed story. In "Gooseberries,"[27] Ivan and Bourkin are out hunting on an overcast day. Bourkin on the first page reminds Ivan that the latter had previously offered to tell a story. Instead of presenting the story, the narrator keeps us in the frame situation, moving with the men to the house of their friend Aliokhin, who employs the pretty maid Pelagueya. The men bathe exuberantly, swim, change, and settle down in the comfortable farmhouse living room to tea and jam brought them by the girl. ". . . only then did Ivan Ivanich begin his story" (p. 44). The story is about happiness.

> "We are two brothers," he began, "I, Ivan Ivanich, and Nicholai Ivanich, two years younger. I went in for study and became a veterinary surgeon, while Nicholai was at the Exchequer court when he was nineteen . . ."

So much could be the beginning of a story, a story that stands on its own without the context of a frame. The story that Ivan tells is an interesting one, one that raises moral questions and constantly reminds us that life needs to be explained. There are numerous possible meanings for this story, but we need not enumerate them, for Chekov draws our attention back to the context again and again to keep us from going off into irrelevant speculations about Nicholai. When, in the telling, Ivan begins relating what seem to him to be parallels to his theme, he is interrupted—

"Keep to your story," said Bourkin (p. 47)

and the context of the frame is revivified. Such bits, small as a single line, can easily recall whole contexts if those contexts were themselves made clear. Empirical studies of word recall[28] conclude that contexts can be recalled ever more vividly, and with ever smaller stimuli, as their traces are activated more frequently. The line of interruption is a simple plot device to remind us that our concern is less with the story of Nicholai than with the larger tale. Such reminders may be part of the narration rather than the plot:

"After the death of his wife," Ivan Ivanich continued, after a long pause . . . (p. 47).

The section not in quotation marks reminds us that there is a narrator, someone with his own purposes, who is mediating between us and Ivan, reminding us of the larger story. Ivan, too, is a narrator mediating between his tale and his auditors: Bourkin, Aliokhin, and us. The style of his narration reminds us that he too has his purposes. "I want to tell you what a change took place in me in those few hours I was in his house" (p. 50). Such a style on Ivan's part serves to remind us that our concern is with the larger story; it shifts our attention from statement to expression; it continuously revivifies the frame (which is a context) and forces us to understand Nicholai's story as part of

27

the whole of "Gooseberries." From the standpoint of
the on-going structure—the existence of the frame-to-
be-completed—the plot and the style function iden-
tically. Bits of plot and bits of style both make
procontextual comparisons that constantly remind us
what we are about.

Nicholai's story, alone, is about forcefully taking
happiness, about his love of gooseberries. His refrain
is "How good they are!" Ivan's problem, however,
comes from his inability to understand his brother.
For him the gooseberries become the emblem (he
says) of immoral hedonism. But for us the complex of
the two becomes a story in which we see the poignancy
of the conflict between one's view of the givens of life,
and one's aspirations about one's life. "Gooseberries"
goes back into the frame story, puts all the men to
bed, and ends as "the rain beat against the windows
all night long" (p. 54). The symbol of the berries
works in both contexts, the central story and the
frame, to support procontextually certain meanings.
The enterprise of the story is to make gooseberries into
a double metaphor through recontextualization.
Although Melville's description of the lee shore (p. 20)
works through alternation of context and Chekov's
narration of gooseberries works through interpolation
of context, they both have the same effect of creating
a double metaphor. And in both, the structure which
holds us suspended is one which works toward some
final unitary conception.

One may be tempted to argue that the importance of context in creating the structure of suspense
is a synchronic phenomenon rather than a diachronic
one. Similarly, one might surmise that context in
examples such as ours, where the parts of the
narrative are so easily separable, is merely a special
case. Both of these objections should be met.

Consider Hawthorne's beautiful tale, "The Great Carbuncle." It begins:

> **At nightfall, once in the olden time, on the rugged side of one of the Crystal Hills, a party of adventurers were refreshing themselves, after a toilsome and fruitless quest for the Great Carbuncle. They had come thither not as friends nor partners in the enterprise, but each, save one youthful pair, impelled by his own selfish and solitary longing for this wondrous gem.**[29]

Already here we see a context building up. We have a setting, a population, and more importantly, the beginning of the subliminal establishment of a value system: the central conjunction *but* is of immense importance. (We also have the narrator's attitude toward his materials conveyed through his choice of tone. The analysis of narrative voice is reserved for a later section.) The context defines two possible ethical camps: the shared and the estranged. "Once" we are on "one" of the hills, with a "party" that divides into two camps, the "not friends" and "not partners" who are "impelled by" their "own selfish and solitary longing" against a "youthful pair." Still on that first page we find "one of their number," "estranged," "solitary," "solitary," "individual," and "one," for "the Great Carbuncle must make them strangers."

Hawthorne describes his personages. The third paragraph begins, "The eldest of the group . . ." and proceeds to physical description and anecdotal characterization. The paragraph proceeds, "Near this miserable Seeker sat a little elderly personage . . ." And then "Another of the adventurers was . . . The fourth whom we shall notice . . . The fifth adventurer likewise . . . The sixth of the party was a young man of haughty mien, and sat somewhat apart from the rest." Through the reading of the paragraph the reader learns a descriptive convention: characters will be introduced singly and, in turn, each particularized by an item of physical detail and a modicum of story.

But the fourth paragraph violates this convention:

> Lastly, there was a handsome youth in rustic garb, and *by his side* a blooming little person, in whom a delicate shade of maiden reserve was just melting into the rich glow of a young *wife's affection*. Her name was Hannah, and her husband's Matthew; *two* homely names, yet well enough adapted to the simple *pair*, who seemed strangely out of place among the whimsical fraternity whose wits had been set agog by the Great Carbuncle. [Emphasis mine.]

Here we have one short paragraph standing against the long third paragraph of introductions, two characters described at once, as opposed to the serial description of the others. The radical disjunction between Hannah and Matthew and their fellow adventurers is established here not only by their simplicity, but by the unexpectedly short paragraph giving an unexpectedly double description. This is a diachronic effect and it depends upon context. Notice how the very sentence structure reproduces in miniature the temporal structure of the story:

1. **Her name was Hannah,** and
2. **her husband's Matthew;**
3. **two homely names,**
4. **yet well enough adapted to the simple pair,**
5. **who seemed strangely out of place among the whimsical fraternity whose wits had been set agog by the Great Carbuncle.**

1 is directly joined to 2 by the uncompromising *and.* Both begin with *her.* Both end with a proper name.

The necessity of seeing these two clauses as a unit is reinforced by making the reading of 2 depend upon the reader's unconscious appropriation of the verb from 1. We can also note that both 1 and 2 are five syllables long. This unit (1+2) must be taken together in order to supply an antecedent for *two* in 3. Similarly, *the* of *the . . . pair* in 4 requires an antecedent which can only be 1+2. Thus, 3 and 4 are joined in their reference. However, unlike 1 and 2, 3 and 4 do not share the same grammatical structure; though metrically separable, they work together as a logical union of two elements (*homely* and *simple*) created by the connective *yet*. Thus 3+4 makes a unit which by reference becomes one with 1+2. This newly created larger unit stands all together in opposition to 5, a unit which cannot be broken down in the way 1+2+3+4 was because of the relativizing pronouns *who* and *whose*. The reference of 5, of course, is to the six characters of the preceding long paragraph. Thus, the assertion of the shared unity of Matthew and Hannah stands metrically, grammatically, and referentially opposed to the world of the estranged. The movement within this sentence mirrors the larger movement from the third to the fourth paragraph, and we see that the synchronic opposition implied in the first lines of the story in fact comes to life when it is embodied diachronically; the context here, though not at all separable in the way a central story is from its frame, controls the development of meaning with exactly the same pervasive force.

The story goes on to present the conversation of the adventurers. Each in turn relates his aspirations for the Great Carbuncle. One wishes to embrace it and die; one to destroy it in the course of chemical and physical analysis; one to hoard it for its financial value; one to hide it as a private source of inspiration;

one to grace his family hall with it, a family of which he is the last living member; one to disprove its existence. And, indeed, the gem is narratively susceptible to these uses; that is, it supports each of the characters metaphorically. But all these stand against Matthew and Hannah.

> "Ye must know, friends, that Hannah and I, being wedded the last week, have taken up the search of the Great Carbuncle, because we shall *need* its light . . . such a pretty thing to *show the neighbors* . . . It will shine through the house so that . . . when we awake in the night, to be able to see *one another's faces!*" [Emphasis mine.]

The camp of the estranged, of the one, begins to take on the additional negative values of destruction and waste; while the shared, the two, takes on the added positive value of use. This accretion of value occurs through the diachronic perception of bits which flesh out metaphorically the very context that has been established from the first line. The system of evaluative dichotomies continues to grow around the basic distinction between estranged and shared. Referring to one of the characters, the Cynic, the narrator says:

> He was one of those wretched and evil men whose yearnings are downward to the darkness, instead of heavenward . . . the lights which God hath kindled for us . . .

The use of *one* versus *us* revivifies the context within which we have been working. Now the two sides of the dichotomy are expanded to include downness, darkness, and evil on the side of the one; and upness, light, and good on the side of the two. At this point in our argument, however, we are not so much describing style, or narrative structure, as thematic development.

This same temporal process is apparent in Hawthorne's characterization. When, the morning after the characters have told their motives, Matthew and Hannah are climbing the hills on their search, they exchange the following remarks:

> "Let us climb up a little higher," whispered she, yet tremulously, as she turned her face upward to the lonely sky.
>
> "Come, then," said Matthew, mustering his manly courage and drawing her along with him, for she became timid again the moment that he grew bold.

One character waxes as the other wanes and vice versa. The mutuality of the two reinforces their entire context that depends so heavily on words such as "two," "pair," "mutual," and "conjugal." This sharing of effort as they climb functions in the plot in the same way that the young couple's shared view of "one another's faces" functions in the development of theme.

At this point in "The Great Carbuncle," we are set up for, waiting for, suspended for, Matthew and Hannah finding the gem before all the others. This would, of course, be in keeping with the value system that has been established. But we would be disappointed by such an ending as we are disappointed by a mystery story whose *denouement* we perceive too early in our reading.

Although it is too lengthy to reprint here, the ending, the last four pages, is well worth rereading. The couple stand beside a haze-covered lake. They perceive an ever-growing light. Suddenly, they see, or think they see, the Great Carbuncle. Across the lake, atop a precipice, the gem radiates light. A figure, or an optical illusion, is climbing there before them. It is the old man, the one who wished to die. But perhaps not, for, as they begin to make out the figure, they see that it is immobile, turned to stone, forever a part of the rock face, ever reaching toward the summit.

"It is the Seeker," whispered Hannah, convulsively grasping her husband's arm. "Matthew, he is dead."

"The joy of success has killed him," replied Matthew, trembling violently. "Or, perhaps, the very light of the Great Carbuncle was death!"

The other characters arrive on the scene, yet each has an imperfect vision of the stone, the Cynic's so imperfect that he gets no glimpse at all. Matthew and Hannah are the only ones to see it clearly, but the sight convinces them not to try to possess it. The haze re-forms.

There is much in this final vision that reminds one of Moses allowed to see only God's back from the cleft of the mountain, or the blinding flash that converted Saint Paul. "Perhaps the very light of the Great Carbuncle was death!" The dichotomies that have progressively weighted the context up to the ending imply the moral superiority of Matthew and Hannah over their fellows. This implication, however, is not in some simple manner carried out by awarding the gem to the couple. Rather, no one gets the stone. We are suddenly reminded that the gem itself is a *one,* and though men who strive to overcome their selfish, individual isolation are more fit to see the stone than the self-seekers, by virtue of its unity (a projection of the divine infinity) the Carbuncle cannot be possessed. The theological aspects of the context created by the light and darkness imagery are suddenly brought forward as the last bits of the tale further modulate its total impact. In the last paragraph, the narrator says:

Some few believe that this inestimable stone is blazing as of old, and say that they have caught its radiance, like a flash of summer lightning, far down the valley of the Saco. And be it owned that, many a mile from the Crystal Hills, I saw a wondrous light around their summits, and was lured, by the faith of poesy, to be the latest pilgrim of the Great Carbuncle.

The theologic values are revived by "radiance," "light," "faith," and "pilgrim." But suddenly the whole is thrown radically into a temporal context, the narrator injecting himself overtly into the tale to bring it down to the time of writing. We realize that the *one* and the *two* are parallel to the *then* and the *now*. On reexamination, we notice that all the serial descriptions began with the oldest and proceeded to the youngest. The tales of motives were similarly organized. The couple are the youngest seekers. And we see a narrator who is the latest pilgrim. He is drawn by the faith of *poesy,* and it is not amiss to point out that the problem in narrative, necessarily a temporal medium, is to construct a unity that will be the tale. The narrator's search, in some real sense, constitutes his writing of "The Great Carbuncle," an enterprise that attempts to unite, as we wait suspended, the one and the two, the estranged and the shared, the form and the content, the development of theme, character, and time, and the whole with the process of writing and the process of reading. All of the views we may take of narrative which conserve its temporal nature profit by analysis in terms of context and bits. The assertion that "context is the complete perceptual freight that we must bring with us to understand the significance of a bit as we perceive it" (p. 22) implies a whole notion of our engagement with the on-going narrative. Context is a momentary view of a developmental phenomenon, a phenomenon to which we are subliminally attuned. It is this very phenomenon that creates the reality of fiction.

Fictional Reality

Books, even (or especially) the books that curricula seem to honor, often fail for some individuals. This is a loss. But when a book does not fail, when the reader has gone driving through of his own accord, that book has worked strange magic. Suddenly it becomes easy to talk about "the world" of that book, or the loss of one's self to the experience, or identification with some character. This magic is worked subliminally. We never stop, consider the implications of the world of the book, and then decide, quite rationally, that we will accept that world. We needn't go through such defensive maneuvers because we all know that the book will eventually be over. Did we not know this, I doubt that many people would read books; certainly, few people would become addicted to reading *per se,* going from one book to another without even knowing about the books in advance. But people are so addicted; they must enjoy the experience of reading. "Tell me a story."

The abandon with which children approach narrative has impelled countless students of the problem of fictional reality to look to the young for answers to questions about the dynamics of our response to reading. I believe that this approach has much to offer. Some may say that we are not children, but we all have been children, and it has left a permanent mark on us. E. M. Forster[30] says that, when the world no longer demands of him that he be a brilliant and astute critic, he will retire to his room to read and reread *The Swiss Family Robinson.* This seems to me a boring, but highly understandable, enterprise.

When we read as critics, we make ourselves free in the world of criticism, and the book becomes an object. When we read as readers, we make ourselves free in the world of the book.

Lionel Trilling's[31] notion of the mithridatic function of literature (in which we read and read, always about the same trauma, until we can come to grips with that trauma) seems useful. In questioning my students and colleagues I have found that almost everyone through his life develops his literary background genre by genre. For me, it was science fiction from age ten to age twelve, then adventure from twelve to thirteen, and mysteries the following summer. Such predilections imply a desire to abdicate discussion of a problem to someone else, a narrator. Perhaps Forster knows that his choice of the intellectual life will always seem to him a hard one, that there was once a possibility of an adventurous innocence which he spurned. And so in his old age he will re-create it again and again. But perhaps not. We need not psychoanalyze Forster to assert, with Bachelard, that "to read . . . is essentially to daydream."[32]

Norman Holland tries to do more than locate our ruling trauma and identify it with our favorite genre. He makes an interesting case[33] that the work of literature is a transformation (psychic structure) that manipulates for us our infantile fantasies. This obviates the necessity for us to grapple with any unpleasant implications of such fantasies. We shift the responsibility onto the literature. Thus, our psyche, by investing in the literature, gets a return in the form of freedom from *self*-control. (Essentially, this conforms to the orthodox Freudian theory of psychic economy.) Holland goes on to assert, still in a rather orthodox manner, that we all share similar infantile fantasies. Therefore, we can say that the best and most enduring books are the ones that serve the most people at the most times as the most effective transformation. However, we know (certainly since Erikson)[34] that passing from one psychological stage of development to another need not be traumatic and that, since certain fantasies are, as the psychologists put it, specific for fixation at a certain stage, not all people feel drawn, for purposes of personal psychic economy, to all fantasies. And yet I have never found anyone who approached *Don Quixote* after graduating high school who did not enjoy it. I think the addiction to reading must lie in something more general than ontogeny and less specific than genre.

"The names provided by parents for children anticipate the functional structure of the child's world."[35] Children are told to call a certain individual, "Father," not "man," or "Robert," or "Bob," or, as the mother might, "Darling." Each of these names is, of course, correct. But each implies a different "functional structure." R. Brown has tested this thesis against the other extant theories of naming. The conclusion of his study is worth citation:

> Though we often think of each thing as having a name—a single name—in fact, each thing has many equally correct names. When some thing is named for a child, adults show considerable regularity in their preference for one of the many possible names. This paper is addressed to the question: "What determines the name given to a child for a thing?" The first answer is that adults prefer the shorter to the longer expression. This gives way to the frequency principle. Adults give a thing the name it is most commonly given. We have now come full circle and are left with the question,

"Why is one name for a thing more common than another?"
It seems likely that things are first named so as to categorize them in a maximally useful way. For most purposes Referent A is a spoon rather than a piece of silverware, and Referent B a dime rather than a metal object. The same referent may have its most useful categorization on one level (*Prince*) for one group (the family) and on another level (*dog*) for another group (strangers). The categorization that is most useful for very young children (*money*) may change as they grow older (*dime* and *nickel*).

With some hierarchies of vocabulary the more concrete terms are learned before the abstract; probably the most abstract terms are never learned first, but it often happens that a hierarchy develops in both directions from a middle level of abstraction. Psychologists who believe that mental development is from abstract to the concrete, from a lack of differentiation, have been embarrassed by the fact that vocabulary often builds in the opposite direction. This fact need not trouble them, since the sequence in which words are acquired is not determined by the cognitive preferences of children so much as by the naming practices of adults.[36]

In exactly the same manner, our access to the verbal construct which is the world of a narrative is not determined by our preferences, but by the habits of narrators. And narrators, like parents, name things according to their own notions of maximal utility, a practice which defines the functional structure of the world of their narrative.

Consider the beginning of *The Wings of the Dove:*

She waited, Kate Croy, for her father to come in, but he kept her unconscionably, and there were moments at which she showed herself, in the glass over the mantel, a face positively pale with the

irritation that had brought her to the point of going away without sight of him.[37]

We know, of course, that we have met this character at a moment of crisis: she is about to leave. This crisis is in some sense parallel to a crisis in her relation with her father, for, though she seems to be leaving voluntarily, she is forcing herself to see him, a man whom, we would assume, she always has sufficient grace to see. But we also know, within the narrator's frame of reference at this point, that Kate Croy is more important than her father to the story. After all, were it the other way around, we would have found *Croy's daughter waiting for him,* a significant variation in wording. We also know the relation between the two characters. First we have the assertion that one is the father to the other. This implies a host of things to people who have known fathers, and all of us have. But the estrangement between them makes this a more specific filial relation, one of tension. Thus, the second clause recontextualizes the notion of father to define the functional structure yet more specifically. In addition, we learn from this opening that, regardless of the fact that Kate is more central to the story than her father is, the narrator feels none too close to her: he refers to her by her full name. He could just as easily have called her *Kate,* and had the father come in as *Mr. Croy.* Full names imply a certain formality in English, and the narrator, by tuning in to this, further constitutes the literary world by beginning to establish his relation to his characters as well as their interrelations. But despite this distance, the narrator knows Kate well. After all, he begins with *she,* only remembering an instant later that this pronoun is meaningless to us, since we do not share its antecedent. (Although the use of a first person pronoun for such effect is time honored, it is interesting to note the great vogue of third person pronouns without antecedents in twentieth-century narrative.)[38] Thus, the very words that create and modulate the context within which bits of information appear are the words that determine a functional structure for the world of the narrative. We may, on an abstract moral or philosophical level, reject this world, but, if we intend to read the book, at a subliminal level we must understand and accept it.

It is just this subliminal acceptance (of the notion *earlier*) that causes despair for the parents of a college student who receive a night-letter that says, "Please ignore earlier telegram." It is the fundamental involvement with the world of the command that makes it impossible for us to comply with the order, "For the next three minutes, do not think about elephants." Of course, we can obey the command by consciously deciding to think about giraffes or by reading something unrelated. However, in narrative we are not allowed the latter solution, and we cannot proceed in our reading if we opt for the former.

It is one of the insights of both modern grammar[39] and symbolic logic[40] that that which we most fundamentally know are identifications and predications. Consider the famous sentence, "Scott wrote *Waverley*." *Wrote* implies the possibility of a two-place predicate (in this case, a writer related to a written); it also implies the possibility of the existence of a past time. *Scott* implies the possibility of there being someone named Scott; and this further implies the possibility of there being someone. *Waverly* implies the possibility of the existence of something named Waverley; and this further implies the possibility of there being something. When we read "Scott wrote *Waverley*," we say either, "Yes, he did," which is correct, or, "No, he didn't," which is incorrect. Similarly, in considering the parallel sentence about the much-ignored Czech writer, "Emák wrote *Alphonse*," we either say, "Yes, he did," or, "No, he didn't." However, there never was, to my knowledge, anyone named Emák. Indeed, I don't even know if Emák is a possible Czech name, though I've made free with the diacritical marking. Nonetheless, if we concern ourselves with the truth of "Emák wrote *Alphonse*," we are thrust into the position of accepting the existence of Emák, accepting that he knew how to write, that he did it at a past time, and that someone could write a book, and that it was called *Alphonse*. Similar statements could be made of "Scott did *not* write *Waverley*." When we are concerned at the level of the truth of the assertion of the sentence, we must subliminally accept all the underlying statements of possibility as statements of truth. Anyone who has taught criticism knows how hard it is to train students to see beneath the words themselves to their implications. For me, this argues that our critical abilities, including our ability to assert that, "ah yes, Emák never existed, so the question of the truth of the proposition is irrelevant," are abilities that are superimposed upon our more fundamental reading experience. And besides, how could one read James at all if one stopped after the fourth word and said, "Kate Croy? There never was a Kate Croy." For the reading of that first sentence, it is much more to the point that we wonder whether "unconscionably," which seems to be Kate's term, is in fact accurate because her father is mean or cruel or thoughtless, or whether, in fact, it is inaccurate, and Kate is misunderstanding a reasonable delay because she is impetuous, egocentric, and inconsiderate.

Were we not to focus on the assertions themselves, but on their underlying implications, literature would be impossible. Don Quixote, so beloved, would be scoffed at as a whim. Fantasy and allegory would be dismissed as untrue. But we never ask truth of literature at this level.

In a hole in the ground there lived a hobbit. Not a nasty, dirty, wet hole, filled with the ends of worms and an oozy smell, nor yet a dry, bare, sandy hole with nothing in it to sit down on or to eat: it was a hobbit-hole, and that means comfort.[41]

Such an abode, by virtue of the nonexistence of hobbits, cannot exist, but who would be cruel enough to dismiss it? No one. And for those who enjoy Tolkien, they not only don't dismiss the vision, they embrace it. His trilogy, for them, is all too short, not because the problems posed in the narrative have not been solved (they have, and neatly), but because finishing the text means leaving its world. Worlds appeal to us for many reasons: their comfort, their excitement, their danger, their curious relations to our own world. Whatever the reason for its appeal, we are drawn back to a good book because of its narrative world. We do not merely think back wistfully, but we reread, because the narrative world is constituted for the reader, as the child's by his parents, through time. It is the process that counts.

However, the concern here is not directly with second readings, but with first readings. Meanings accrue to words in structures by implication. However, meanings arise in narrative from other sources also. Empson[42] unloads as many of these as he can through the amorphous but useful method he calls "verbal analysis." The utility of this method has been exploited largely in the criticism of poetry. I think that it is equally fruitful in a consideration of narrative.

43

Narrative Suspense

The following is a punning passage drawn from *Look Homeward, Angel*.[43] It is amusing in itself, important in Wolfe's characterization, and significant in its placing within the novel. However, rather than analyze it exhaustively, let us use it as an example for "verbal analysis."

1   "Gene!" yelled Harold Gay, hurling a thick
2 volume from him under the spell of Elk's great
3 names. "What do you know about history? Who
4 signed Magna Charta, eh?"
5   "It wasn't signed," said Eugene. "The King
6 didn't know how to write, so they
7 mimeographed it."
8   "Correct!" roared Harold Gay. "Who was
9 Aethelred the Unready?"
10   "He was the son of Cynewulf the Silly and
11 Undine the Unwashed," said Eugene.
12   "On his Uncle Jasper's side," said Elk Dun-
13 can, "He was related to Paul the Poxy and
14 Genevieve the Ungenerous."
15   "He was excommunicated by the Pope in a
16 Bull of the year 903, but he refused to be cowed,"
17 said Eugene.
18   "Instead, he called together all the local
19 clergy, including the Archbishop of Canterbury,
20 Dr. Gay, who was elected Pope," said Elk Dun-
21 can. "This caused a great schism in the
22 Church."
23   "But as usual, God was on the side of the
24 greatest number of canons," said Eugene.

In the course of this passage, the reader first hears the protagonist's name. He is asked about history, essentially a challenge to the youth to place himself. He refuses the challenge. The obvious logical contradiction between mimeographing and inability to write shows us his attitude. Each of the historical figures in the exchanges that follow could easily be used to characterize a rebellious youth: unready, unwashed, ungenerous, not to be cowed. This chatter leads Elk to assert that the historic process, as the roommates discuss it, results in schism. The allusion to the Great Schism of 1054 is obvious and throws the question of one's relation to history into a realm of the spirit. After this passage, of course, we see Eugene's lonely life at the university which leads to his running away altogether, smitten with war fever. This movement of the passage is obvious even to a reader unaware of the references. (Schism is such an unusual word that most people encounter it only in the phrase *Great Schism.* If a reader does not know one, he will not know the other. If the lower case letters were to throw this uneducated reader off, the dictionary, which lists Great Schism with schism itself, will set him straight.)

The method of analysis that we have followed so far would indicate, however, that such a description of the effect of the passage is insufficient. We would want to note, for example, that the ironic disjunction between *write* and *mimeographed* or of *Bull* and *cowed* structurally mimic the movement from history to schism and parallel Eugene's growing alienation. (Empson, on the other hand, would have us look for allusions, "any verbal nuance, however slight, which gives room for alternative reactions to the same piece of language."[44] This, of course, is Empson's definition of ambiguity.) Let us work through the passage:

1 *Gene **makes a Klang association with a girl's name.**
 Harold **was the name of a number of significant medieval rulers.**
 *Gay **suggests, mildly, homosexuality.**
 *hurling **is a game.**
2 *Elk's **suggests the name of the famous fraternal association.**

4 *Charta* **is the disfavored spelling.**

9 *Aethelred* **comes from a root meaning** *noble.*
  Unready **is actually a mistranslation of** *unraed,*
  which means *uncouncilled.*

10 *****The alliteration implied in** *son of Cynewulf the*
  Silly **is actually illegitimate, because the "c" of**
  Cynewulf **is hard.**

11 ***Undine,* **refers to the mythical sea-nymph, who**
  cannot be called *unwashed.*

12 **A** *Jasper* **is a dupe in older American slang.**
  ***Jasper* **is a type of colored quartz.**

16 *Bull* **has a special use, in slang, as** *bullshit.*
  903 **was one of the years in which both a pope**
  (Leo V) and an anti-pope (Christopher) were
  elected.

19 **Becket,** *Archbishop of Canterbury,* **died actually**
  as a result of a feud about separation of church
  and state.

20 *Dr. Gay* **recalls** *Dr. Arbuthnot* **and** *John Gay,* **two**
  Protestant friends and collaborators of the
  Roman Catholic Alexander Pope.

I have not mentioned the most accessible allusions, e.g., the relation between the Magna Carta and personal freedom. Such allusions clearly support the context and help to enrich an already understandable passage. The analysis of this passage would proceed nicely, but incompletely, under the method of examining the structural implications behind the words themselves (as with the James passage, p. 39) and the syntax in which they occur (as with the sentence from Hawthorne, p. 30). Obviously, this passage asks us to bring to bear knowledge beyond the first dictionary definition of the word. Most of these abstruse allusions above operate, as do the more obvious allusions, to reinforce and enrich the passage. But some, those which are starred, seem to require extreme critical gymnastics to be integrated into the passage. (It is the existence of those allusions that prompts Empson to call nuances "ambiguities." However, as our minds skip past irrelevant uses for a parable, they skip past irrelevant associations with a word. These associations do not create ambiguity because, excluded by the context, they do not enter our reading.)

Nonetheless, legitimate allusion is clearly a potent force for creating the reality of the fiction. Unlike words themselves, however, associations with proper names are useful only to an audience whose education includes those proper names. This idea of audience education holds not only for the common associations with names, but the less common allusion present in quotations, stylistic parody, and so forth. Since so much of what has been called allusion does not contribute to our reading, it is fortunate that we read an allusion into our experience of the work only when something else in the work indicates that that is a proper procedure.

If the allusion supports a complete parody (say *Shamela* parodying *Pamela*) the apprehension of an allusive structure is integral, though so saying implies the necessary limitation of the intended audience (to people who have read *Pamela*). If the allusion is conveyed through style, it will work subliminally for an audience familiar with the referred-to style (e.g., narrative passages that appropriate the style of the King James Bible). But, generally speaking, though allusion adds to a passage, the passage must be able to support the allusion. That is, the reality of the fictional world must be communicable without reference to history, literature, and so forth.

Let me stress one point. I am not discounting the importance of allusion; the whole field of literary parody is based on it. Rather, I am asserting that the *meaning* of the allusion is not fundamental to realizing the fiction. What is essential is the knowledge that allusion is being *used*. *Incognita* is written in a style that seems to descend, by conscious imitation, from *Euphues.* Knowing this is of great help to a student of the history of style; it has no realizing force for the reader of *Incognita.* On the other hand, when Dekker writes, "It is now about eighteen years past since a bed of strange snakes were found,"[45] although the allusion is abstruse, we are influenced by the knowledge that Dekker's narrator feels himself placed within a tradition. The reader of Wolfe need not remember the details of the Magna Carta and the Great Schism. What he must acknowledge is that Wolfe's narrator feels such references have a place in his story.

Of course, the more common the allusion is, the more firmly it becomes part of the very fabric of the story. References to the Bible are clearly accessible to most readers. Thus, a reader of *The Sound and the Fury* is likely to respond immediately to the knowledge that Benjy, the articulate/inarticulate idiot, was castrated by his family, through lack of understanding, at the age of thirty-three. Similarly, one would expect that someone who takes the trouble to read Joyce would have sufficient knowledge of literature to immediately perceive the possible significances of Dedalus. To speak of allusion working in this immediate manner, however, is not to track down the nuances (as Empson advises), but to claim something about the education of the reader.

More important for a discussion of the sources of fictional reality are the notions of phenomenology. We may have missed Dedalus in our reading, but, as Merleau-Ponty[46] tells us, we are hardly likely to have missed living with our bodies in the world. We have all learned to organize space around our pervasive subliminal knowledge of our bodies. Thus, we find no difficulty in thinking of Achilles as a tall warrior. It avails little to claim that tall, by Homer's standards, was probably about five foot six. The use of *tall* puts us into a phenomenological context whose truth we assent to regardless of the facts of physical biology.

Gaston Bachelard has shown the amazing regularity with which certain phenomena are appropriated by literature for certain purposes only.[47] It is not useful here to recount all of his insights, anymore than it is useful to describe the functional structure implied in all words. What we should note, however, is that words imply, besides a functional structure, a phenomenal structure. Thus, high and low almost always function as moral attributes. So do light and dark (as we have seen in Hawthorne). Intimate space is always reassuring; subterranean is eerie; unbounded is frightening. Attics are of the intellect; cellars of the viscera. We have all learned to attach certain emotional states to certain phenomena. Fire, for example, is a marvelous phenomenon which, according to Bachelard, functions in any one of four separate syndromes, each syndrome mapping out a range of emotions. Rivers could be equally studied. It is astounding that the difficulties of the Bundren family in burying Addie seem, as they struggle against the river, to support Heraclitus's notions, even though Faulkner was not overtly making reference to the philosopher.[48] James begins *The Turn of the Screw* with the following sentence:

> **The story had held us, round the fire, sufficiently breathless, but except the obvious remark that it was gruesome, as, on Christmas Eve in an old house a strange tale should essentially be, I**

> **remember no comment uttered till somebody
> happened to say that it was the only case he had
> met in which such a visitation had fallen on a
> child.**[49]

It strikes me that we trust the narrator when he
assures us that the tale is "gruesome." We shouldn't,
for we have not had time to develop trust in him at
this point (other than that we at first grant any
narrator), and we have certainly not heard the story
for ourselves. But how, after all, could a tale told
"round a fire" by a group on a wintry night *not* be
gruesome?[50] This is the longest night of the year.

But we need to go beyond the phenomenologists'
attack on single phenomena. "The story held us" tells
us that it was suspenseful in a way that we expect the
tale we will read to be suspenseful. So does
"breathless"; we all know what kind of "breathless"
this is, and it is clearly not the breathlessness
following a long sprint. "Old house" conjures up
demons regardless of the fact that we may not place
the phrase as part of the trappings of ghost tales, for,
at this point, we may not have consciously realized
that James is playing with the conventions of the
ghost tale. But subliminally, he has already placed us
within the ghost tale itself.

Fire, then, along with *river* and *old house* and a
host of other things that we all grew up with, imply
phenomenal structures. Although we are not consciously aware of these, practiced psychologists can
see beyond them to the constitution of the mind that
uses them. The following should give a brief notion of
the complexity with which houses can be invested by
(especially) the minds that do not analyze them.

> **All great, simple images reveal a psychic state. The
> house . . . is a "psychic state," and even when**

reproduced as it appears from the outside, it bespeaks intimacy. Psychologists . . . have studied the drawings of houses made by children, and even used them for testing. Indeed, the house-test has the advantage of welcoming spontaneity, for many children draw a house spontaneously while dreaming over their pencil and paper. To quote Anne Balif: "Asking a child to draw his house is asking him to reveal the deepest dream shelter he has found for his happiness. If he is happy, he will succeed in drawing a snug, protected house which is well built on deeply-rooted foundations." . . . the right shape, and nearly always there will be some indication of its inner strength. In certain drawings, quite obviously . . ."it is warm indoors, and there is a fire burning, such a big fire, in fact, that it can be seen coming out of the chimney." When the house is happy, soft smoke rises in gay rings above the roof.

If the child is unhappy, however, the house bears traces of his distress. In this connection, I recall that Francoise Minkowska organized an unusually moving exhibition of drawings by Polish and Jewish children who had suffered during the last war. One child, who had been hidden in a closet every time there was an alert, continued to draw narrow, cold, closed houses long after those evil times were over . . . houses that have become motionless in their rigidity. "This rigidity and motionlessness are present in the *smoke* as well as in the window curtains. The surrounding trees are quite *straight* and give the impression of standing guard over the house." Mme. Minkowska knows that a live house is not really "motionless," that, particularly, it integrates the movements by means of which one accedes to the door. Thus the path that leads to the house is often a climbing one. At times, even, it is inviting. In any case, it always possesses certain kinesthetic features. If we were taking a

51

> Rorschach test, we should say that the house has
> "K."
> Often a simple detail suffices for Mme.
> Minkowska . . . to recognize the way the house
> functions. In one house, drawn by an eight-year-
> old child, she notes that there is "a knob on the
> door; people go in the house, they live there." It is
> not merely a constructed house, it is also a house
> that is "lived-in." Quite obviously the door-knob
> has a functional significance. This is the
> kinesthetic sign, so frequently forgotten in the
> drawings of "tense" children.
> Naturally, too, the door-knob could hardly be
> drawn in scale with the house, its function taking
> precedence over any question of size. For it
> expresses the function of opening, and only a
> logical mind could object that it is used to close as
> well as to open the door.[51]

For this child's mind, the out-size doorknob
dominates the image. In the beginning of James's
novella, the fire dominates the image. Of course, we
know that there are chairs, floor, and even somewhere
a kitchen, but our attention is directed to a single
phenomenon, and that phenomenon, in that context,
carries with it emotive value. Fire could have other
emotive values. If, instead of forcing it as the center of
attention for a winter's eve group of tale tellers,
James, with American film directors of the 1940s and
early 1950s, had put it as a rising flame at the end of a
seductive conversation, the fire would have carried
the heat of sexuality. But, as with any allusion to
knowledge that the reader brings to the text, we are
never confused by the irrelevant significances of the
image. In *The Turn of the Screw,* we do not confuse
the fire of hell with the fire of sex or the fire of intellect. This functioning of the phenomenon in context (the general statement of the working of allusion)

gives us a bridge from the notion of the functional structure implied by words back to the temporal notion of narrative. Our words, which provide functional structure, in fact also provide a phenomenal structure whose correct reading is dependent upon the subliminal awareness of the ongoing context.

In this regard, we should mention what I would call the "thunderhead effect." We have learned of certain signs that they not only accompany certain emotional states, but that they precede them. There is Ibsen's famous assertion that one cannot place a gun on stage in the first act and then not have it go off by the end of the third. When there is a thunderhead in fiction, as in our nonliterary lives, we look toward a coming storm.

> **One morning in December, as he was on his way to his lecture on procedure, he thought he noticed more animation than usual in the rue Saint-Jacques. The students were hurrying out of the cafes, or calling to one another from house to house through the open windows. The shopkeepers stood in the middle of the pavement, watching uneasily; shutters were being closed; and, when he reached the rue Soufflot, he saw a large crowd assembled round the Pantheon.**[52]

In this passage from Flaubert, we sense impending communal disaster in the actions of the people. Following this description, a minor riot does occur. Because of what we have learned, then, words (and the images focused through them) imply a functional structure of the fictional world, a phenomenal structure of the fictional world, and a nexal structure ("thunderhead effect") of the fictional world. We must assent to these implications if we are to read, and the reading process obliges us to select the structural implication that helps constitute the world of the narrative.

Let us call these structures, because of their sources, image-structures. Image-structures, as we have seen, must be assented to. They derive definition from context. But context itself depends upon structural considerations. We have the isocolons in Melville, the antitheses in Hawthorne, the balanced style of James. Each of the possible syntaxes also forces us to assent to notions about the constitution of the fictional world. We have already seen this in numerous examples. Rather than go back, let us look at some new ones.

> I wish either my father or my mother, or indeed both of them, as they were in duty both equally bound to it, had minded what they were about when they begot me; had they duly considered how much depended upon what they were then doing;—that not only the production of a rational Being was concerned in it, but that possibly the happy formation and temperature of his body, perhaps his genius and the very cast of his mind;—and, for aught they knew to the contrary, even the fortunes of his whole house might take their turn from the humours and dispositions which were then uppermost;—Had they duly weighed and considered all this, and proceeded accordingly,—I am verily persuaded I should have made a quite different figure in the world from that in which the reader is likely to see me.[53]

This is a typical Shandean sentence; the first, in fact. It is long, disjointed, and, surprisingly, periodic: it works through (Lockean) association in order to amass more and more relevant material until the whole assemblage discharges on the narrative "me." This particular type of discharging of context, induced by the periodicity,[54] is structurally analogous to the whole world of Shandy, in which circumstances marshall themselves, one after the other, to come crashing down upon humanity, in the guise of the windowsash that circumcises the infant Tristram, for example. As opposed to the image-structure that we have considered above, these observations are intended to elucidate a syntax-structure, a structure which we find not only in the sentences, but in the plot (and, as it turns out, in the theme, character-development, and so forth). A vocabulary for more exacting description of syntax structures will be developed in the second chapter of this study. Here let us simply note how various they can be, and how well they work within the whole of the fiction in which we find them. Compare the first sentence of *Tristram Shandy* with the first sentence of *Absalom, Absalom!*[55]

> [1]From a little after two oclock until almost sundown of the long still hot weary dead September afternoon they sat in what [2]Miss Coldfield still called [3]the office[1] because her father had called it that[2]—a[4]dim hot airless room with the blinds all closed and fastened [3]for forty-three summers because when she was a girl someone had believed that light and moving air carried heat and that dark was always cooler, and [5]which ([6]as the sun shone fuller and fuller on that side of the house[6]) became latticed with yellow slashes full of dust motes [4]which Quentin thought of as being [7]flecks of the dead old dried paint itself [5]blown inward from the scaling blinds as wind might have blown them.[7]

This sentence too is long and strangely connected, but hardly periodic. Rather, it is an interlocking structure of sentence within sentence, sentence overlapping sentence. The numbers which I have inserted are intended to mark sentences (by which I mean, minimally, identification and predication), complete sentences falling between the first and second occurrence of the number. In order to read the entire sentence, we must subliminally accept the structural notion on which it is based. This interlocking, overlapping principle in fact is reflected in the method of multiple overlayed narration that Faulkner employs in *Absalom, Absalom!* and the constant effort to get to the heart of the thought behind the sentence is much like the constant effort of the narrators to get to the heart of their tale, the central, untold story of Thomas Sutpen. The structural similarities between the manner of multiple narration and the style may be called, in opposition to image-structure, syntax-structure. Both image-structure and syntax-structure cooperate to foist the fictional reality subliminally on the reader.

However, once we recognize the interdependence of these types of structures, we suddenly realize that we have never left the type of analysis used above to discuss the relationship between metaphor and irony. These also are structural phenomena that derive their power through time. That is, we sense a structure to be completed (even such a simple one as the structure of internal conventions in *The Great Carbuncle*) and we wait suspended for the completion. Both image-structures and syntax-structures can be completed either pro- or anticontextually. A more precise vocabulary will be developed below. Here, let us take note, though, of the cooperative nature of the temporal aspects of narrative.

Consider the famous opening line of *Pride and Prejudice*:

It is a truth universally acknowledged, that a

single man in possession of a good fortune, must be
in want of a wife.[56]

Wife is an obviously anticontextual bit. After all,
at least some *single man,* the image-structure implies
as it builds the context, disagrees by the very
phenomenon of his existence, which denies the
relational term *wife.* The nexal structure, dependent
upon *want,* meaning need, presumably to be fulfilled,
already predicts the movement of the entire book
toward marriage, thus creating the larger structure
which we wait to have fulfilled. However, by virtue of
the anticontextuality of the last bit, we may safely
guess that the book will in some way undercut the
idea that a man is seeking a wife. (Of course, the book
actually turns out to be about Elizabeth's lack of a
husband, a direct reversal of the semantic features.)
The functional structure, on the other hand, implies
(and we must assent to) the possibility of universal
truth and wifedom. Both prove to be the case and
operate against other structures to maintain an anticontextuality that gives the book its ironic tone.
Jane Austen said she tried to work in "two square
inches of ivory,"[57] a small and perfect universe. And
indeed, considering the irony of this first sentence,
what a universe that is! The progress of the sentence
recontextualizes *universe* in order to redefine it as
that world in which said truth operates, the universe
of Austen's bourgeois suburbia. There is in this universe such a thing as a single man. There is such a
thing as a good fortune. And there is such a thing as
that strange truth which the narrator mocks through
irony. We wait now to find out about the single man,
the fortune, and even, though it is undercut, the
truth. The working out of these things, of course, is
manifested in all the levels of the narrative which can
be viewed temporally: the plot, the thematic develop-

ment, the style, the character development. In other words, although far from a mystery story, the first sentence of *Pride and Prejudice* foists structures on the reader's subliminal awareness that keep him in suspense. The world of the fictional reality, as we begin a book, is always a new world, as the whole world is new to a child. Of course the adventure of reading is suspenseful.

Subliminal-Suspense and Plot-Suspense

To understand the kinds of realities we find in books, we must understand the kinds of suspense we feel. We all know what suspense is: it is a part of our lives. It is what we feel when the phone rings in the middle of the night, when a telegram arrives, when a loved one enters the hospital. We feel it before all the tests we face in life: examinations, feats of physical endurance, straining social dilemmas; and before each of the moments of conscious crisis: quitting a job, leaving home, getting married. In *The Sense of an Ending,* Frank Kermode, assuming man's continuing and pervasive interest with eschatology (how things will be after the end) claims that the process of reading a book, as the process of living a life (say, a Christian in A.D. 999 awaiting the millennium), is a dialectic which moves back and forth between "disconfirmation" and "consonance." By this he means that we set up expectations about the shape of the world; but, since the world never does (has) end, the moment of crisis always disconfirms our notions of reality. Then, he continues, the resilient human mind makes some larger pattern, part of which incorporates the world-view and its disconfirmation, part of which makes new predictions which indicate a new end with which our previous disappointment is consonant. When we feel suspense in our lives, these notions of disconfirmation and consonance are applicable, for each of the times we consciously feel suspense is a time that seems to mark the impending end of one state of affairs and the beginning of a new one, the disconfirmation of one world-view, and the learning to live in a new, consonant one. The moments of suspense in our lives have one thing strongly in common with the moments of epochal change that Kermode considers: we take those moments as significant.

When we read a book, we take everything as significant.

We have already discussed how narrators always have purposes of their own. We also know that we never read a narrative without being at least subliminally aware of the presence of the narrator.[58] Narrators do not give us irrelevancies. They may toss in an apparent non sequitur, but that only helps us to hear the timbre of the narrative voice. So, reading, a progress from significance to significance, through disconfirmation and consonance, depends upon suspense. All of the diachronic structures that we have discussed, image-structures and syntax-structures, draw us through a narrative by suspense. This is to reassert the subliminal nature of our engagement with a narrative.

Normally, however, we do not think of subliminal-suspense when we think of suspense. "1. A state or condition of mental uncertainty or excitement, as in awaiting a decision or outcome, usually accompanied by a degree of apprehension or anxiety."[59] When this dictionary definition is applied to literature, we get a statement like this one of M. H. Abrams:

As a plot progresses, it arouses various expectations in the audience or reader about the future

> course of events. **An anxious uncertainty about what is going to happen, especially to those characters with whom we have established bonds of sympathy, is known as** *suspense.*[60]

There is traditional precedent for locating suspense in plot. That is where we have learned to recognize it. But the diachronic structure which is the plot is but one of the diachronic structures which cooperate to create the entire fabric of a narrative. Abrams is referring to the plot-suspense which is most conspicuous in stories of mystery or adventure. Who killed Cock Robin? Can we go to hell *and back?*

The originator of the modern form of these stories is Edgar Allan Poe. The Dupin stories are of especial importance. How, we wonder as the details accumulate, was Marie Roget murdered? How, we ask ourselves again and again, is the purloined letter kept hidden? These are the questions that keep us reading. By an ape! in the first case. By keeping it in an obvious place! in the second. The answers were extraordinary, and extraordinarily satisfying to Poe's audience; they are still sufficient for us. And so we say that the Dupin stories are "good." But compare them to the *Narrative of A. Gordon Pym,*[61] Poe's single attempt at extended narrative.

The young Pym decides to run away from home. A friend arranges that Arthur stow away on a ship on which the friend is signed as cabin-boy. Pym remains locked in a dark hold and there encounters chilling privations. This is all told in the first person, and we can feel Pym's anguish, especially when he is nearly starved and Augustus (the friend) smuggles a note to him instead of releasing him. Arthur is out of matches, but laboriously scrapes together some phosphorous. He is cramped among the stowage and weak from lack of water. His survival may depend upon the contents of the note. He places the scraped phosphorous on the piece of paper and rubs and rubs. There is a brief glow and lo! the paper is blank! Distraught, he tears it to shreds. Only later, having passed out and then regained consciousness, does it occur to Arthur that the writing might have been on the other side of the note. He has no notion of what is going on above deck. He struggles in the pitch black to find the pieces. He painfully fits them together by feel. He ekes out enough phosphorous from the bulkhead for a second try, and gambles that he is now rubbing it into the second side.

> Having rubbed in the phosphorous, a brilliancy ensued as before—but this time several lines of MS. in a large hand, and apparently in red ink, became distinctly visible. The glimmer, although sufficiently bright, was but momentary. Still, had I not been too greatly excited, there would have been ample time enough for me to peruse the whole three sentences before me—for I saw there were three. In my anxiety, however, to read all at once, I succeeded only in reading the seven concluding words, which thus appeared—*"blood—your life depends upon lying close."*
>
> Had I been able to ascertain the entire contents of the note—the full meaning of the admonition which my friend had thus attempted to convey, that admonition, even although it should have revealed a story of disaster the most unspeakable, could not, I am firmly convinced, have imbued my mind with one tithe of the harrowing and yet indefinable horror with which I was inspired by the fragmentary warning thus received. And *"blood,"* too, that word of all words—so rife at all times with mystery, and suffering, and terror—how trebly full of import did it now appear—how chilly and heavily (disjointed, as it thus was, from any foregoing

**words to qualify or render it distinct) did its vague
syllables fall amid the deep gloom of my prison,
into the innermost recesses of my soul! (p. 770)**

Here is suspense. What is going on? What has
happened to Augustus? What will happen to Arthur?
What is the (probably harrowing) context in which
Augustus wrote *"blood"*? Is the "red ink" itself
perhaps blood? This passage strongly builds plot
suspense, and it does so by employing techniques that
engage the reader subliminally in just the way we
have described. There is the separation of the eidetic
context (which remains alive for us) from the
perceived bit which functions within that context.
The sentences are constructed to reinforce this
separation (notice, typically, how the content of the
message is held off, in the last sentence of the first
paragraph, until the very end). The phenomenal
structure is activated by pulling out all stops: the
narrator reports his own excitement, we see *blood,*
and *prison,* and *soul.* The functional structure is
carried by such charged words as *glimmer* and
momentary. The nexal structure runs through the
whole second paragraph with Arthur's fervent wish for
explanation, a wish disappointed by the *disjointed*
words. The message itself is what is most important,
not the story, which is a process. But all of these subliminal effects are clearly being used to create the
plot-suspense.

Arthur does manage finally to get out, only to be
set adrift in the middle of the ocean by a mutinous
crew. He has a series of hair-raising adventures
through the course of which he comes more and more
to realize how wrong he was to leave home. He wants
to go back home, and, since this is a first person
narrative, we are convinced that he did get back
home. After all, the story got into print. So now we are

not only astounded by his ordeals, but waiting (suspended) to see how he gets out of them. Ultimately he is on an oar-less, paddle-less dugout, about fifty feet long, with some other lost sailors and a captive Polynesian savage named Nu-Nu. They have been drawn by irresistible currents into the Antarctic sea (unknown to Poe's readers) which they find "peculiarly free from violent storms or immoderately rough water" (p. 879). They drift on through this placidity noticing only that the coloring of the sea-birds is getting lighter and the ocean's background rumble is growing to a roar. They are on the bottom of the world, and heading for the edge. Arthur keeps a diary record. Suddenly the ocean becomes progressively warmer, and the sky looms more darkly.

March 21st—**A sullen darkness now hovered above us—but from out the milky depth of the ocean a luminous glare arose, and stole up along the bulwarks of the boat. We were nearly overwhelmed by the white ashy shower which settled upon us and upon the canoe, but melted into the water as it fell. The summit of the cataract was utterly lost in the dimness and the distance. Yet we were evidently approaching it with a hideous velocity. At intervals there were visible in it wide, yawning, but momentary rents, and from out these rents, within which was a chaos of flitting and indistinct images, there came rushing and mighty, but soundless winds, tearing up the enkindled ocean in their course.**

March 22nd—**The darkness had materially increased, relieved only by the glare of the water thrown back from the white curtain before us. Many gigantic and pallidly white birds flew continuously now from beyond the veil, and their scream was the eternal *Tekeli-li!* as they retreated from our vision. Hereupon Nu-Nu stirred in the bottom of the boat; but upon touching him, we** found his spirit departed. And now we rushed into the embraces of the cataract, where a chasm threw itself open to receive us. But there arose in our pathway a shrouded human figure, very far larger in its proportions than any dweller among men. And the hue of the skin of the figure was of the perfect whiteness of the snow.

NOTE

The circumstances connected with the late sudden and distressing death of Mr. Pym are already well known to the public through the medium of the daily press. It is feared that the few remaining chapters which were to have completed his narrative, and which were retained by him, while the above were in type, for the purpose of revision, have been irrecoverably lost through the accident by which he perished himself (p. 882).

Now that is begging the question! An editorial note asserts that we know what happened, when of course our very lack of knowledge is what has kept us reading. If the accident to which the editor alludes is the one which the diary foreshadows, then there is no solution we can think of that would have gotten any of the manuscript to the reader. The whole story, at this point, comes to pieces, for an answer is what the plot-suspense had made necessary, and that answer is just what has been left out. Needless to say, *Pym* was not well received in its time and is almost unread today. When we do read it, we read it for the individual episodes, each much like Poe's tales of horror (e.g., "The Tell-Tale Heart"), or we read it for the suspense of the style. The effect of the whole is demolished by the failure to do that which was necessary. There was disconfirmation but no consonance. This is the difference between the Dupin stories and Pym.

However, there are many stories that do not

provide us with the answer we want. *The Lady or the Tiger?* is perhaps the most famous example. The following summary is quite clear:

> **An ancient king invents a court of justice in which prisoners are brought into an arena and made to open one of two doors. Those who open the door behind which is placed a tiger are eaten alive and adjudged guilty; those who open the other find a beautiful lady, marry her, and are adjudged innocent. A youth falls in love with the king's daughter, who returns his love. When he is sentenced to this form of trial, the princess, having discovered the secret of the doors, signals her lover to open the right-hand door. Here the tale ends: "And so I leave it with all of you. Which came out of the opened door—the lady or the tiger?"[62]**

Here there is an answer not given, the answer which the whole story has seemingly made necessary through plot-suspense. But in this case, the withholding of the answer functions to make the very decision a metaphor for justice and for life. It adds something that is in keeping with what has been going on all along: the metaphorization of the unknowable in life. We see then that, although plot-suspense asks for an answer, the presence of that answer is not what makes a story good. What is essential is that a certain kind of necessity be fulfilled. In the Dupin stories, the necessity is fulfilled unusually; in Stockton's dilemma, the necessity is metaphorized; but in Pym, the necessity is substantially ignored.

In most books (adventures, science fiction, adolescent romances, mysteries) there is a strong feeling of necessity, and that necessity is tied to plot-suspense. Suspense, however, need not create a necessity, though it must create a potentiality, a charge. We have already touched on the style of

65

Tristram Shandy (p. 54). The organizing principle behind those periodic sentences adds and adds. Each of the nine books is complete. But adding another does not hurt. In fact, the work was originally published serially between 1760 and 1767. The kind of suspense that operates in Sterne, say between the books, does not create necessity, but potentiality. This may seem like a small distinction, but it actually differentiates, in most books which answer necessity at the end, between the ending of the last chapter and the endings of all the preceding chapters. *Miss Lonelyhearts*[63] provides a good example of the potentiality that can be created by subliminal-suspense.

When the reader opens to the first page of West's work, he does not know whether he is into a novel or a collection of short stories because, instead of a chapter number, he is confronted with a title: "Miss Lonelyhearts, Help me, Help Me." The piece begins:

> **The Miss Lonelyhearts of the New York** *Post-Dispatch* **(Are you in trouble—Do-you-need-advice?—Write-to-Miss-Lonelyhearts-and-she-will-help-you) sat at his desk and stared at a piece of white cardboard (p. 169).**

The nexal structure is already quite clear in the parentheses: the piece is about Miss (hermaphrodite) Lonelyhearts trying to help someone. But there is a problem.

> **. . . he found it impossible to continue. The letters were no longer funny. He could not go on finding the same joke funny thirty times a day for months on end (p. 169).**

The savior is paralyzed. Many readers, I imagine, will find the allusion to Judas's thirty pieces of silver functioning phenomenologically. There is little wonder that Miss Lonelyhearts cannot fulfill his more exalted

role. This, for example, is the first of his letters with
which the reader is presented:

> *Dear Miss Lonelyhearts—*
> *I am in such pain I dont know what to do sometimes*
> *I think I will kill myself my kidneys hurt so much. My*
> *husband thinks no woman can be a good catholic and*
> *not have children irregardless of the pain. I was*
> *married honorably from our church but I never knew*
> *what married life meant as I never was told about man*
> *and wife. My grandmother never told me and she was*
> *the only mother I had but made a big mistake by not*
> *telling me as it dont pay to be inocent [sic] and is only*
> *a big disappointment. I have 7 children in 12 yrs and*
> *ever since the last 2 I have been so sick. I was*
> *operatored [sic] on twice and my husband promised no*
> *more children on the doctors advice as he said I might*
> *die but when I got back from the hospital he broke his*
> *promise and now I am going to have a baby and I don't*
> *[sic] think I can stand it my kidneys hurt so much. I*
> *am so sick and scared because I cant have an abortion*
> *on account of being a catholic and my husband so*
> *religious. I cry all the time it hurts so much and I don't*
> *know what to do.*
>
>

Yours respectfully
Sick-of-it-all (p. 170)

The process of recontextualization that we have discussed before operates to eliminate being "a good
catholic" as a solution to the woman's problems.
Medical help is impossible. Spiritual help is ineffectual. How could one react? "Miss Lonelyhearts threw
the letter into an open drawer and lit a cigarette." The
piece goes on, letter by letter, reaction by reaction,
closing all the possible avenues of effectual help. Miss
Lonelyhearts's boss is Shrike, the mocking city editor.
He comes to check on Miss Lonelyhearts who cannot
complete his column by the deadline.

> "Why don't you give them something new and
> hopeful? Tell them about art. Here, I'll dictate:
> "*Art Is a Way Out.*
> "Do not let life overwhelm you. When the old
> paths are choked with the debris of failure, look for
> newer and fresher paths. Art is just such a path.
> Art is distilled from suffering. As Mr. Polnikoff
> exclaimed through his fine Russian beard, when, at
> the age of eighty-six, he gave up his business to
> learn Chinese, 'We are, as yet, only at the begin-
> ning. . . .'
> "*Art Is One of Life's Richest Offerings.*
> "For those who have not the talent to create,
> there is appreciation. For those . . .
> "Go on from there" (p. 173).

And that is the end of the piece.

Miss Lonelyhearts's inability to go on from there,
paralleling our inability to imagine a true "way out,"
is just the point, in the same way that the withholding
of the answer is the point in *The Lady or the Tiger?*
Unlike Stockton's piece, however, West's goes on.
"We are . . . only at the beginning." Miss
Lonelyhearts later in the work meets real people, not
letters, in need, and fails them, too, a failure that
costs all, so that the last piece ends with his death
(and we are convinced that the collection of short
stories has been a novel). The last-quoted passage is
quite rich. *Offerings* operates both in an existential
and a religious context. *Art* is not only painting, but
the writing of books, like *Miss Lonelyhearts,* or
letters, like those he should write. But these last are
useless, and the narrative proceeds. The suspense set
up by the diachronic structures of this passage is
potential: "Go on from there" could be the last line of
a short story, or (as it is) the entree into the rest of the
novel.

It is important to recognize, however, that, had

Subliminal Knowledge

there been no following novel, or had the last books of
Tristram Shandy not been published, what remained
would still have been a valuable piece of art. This is
not the case when suspense is used to create a necessity, as *Pym* proves to its frustrated readers. Usually,
necessity arises through plot-suspense, but it can arise
through other types of suspense. In James's *Portrait of
a Lady,* for example, we have suspense that depends
upon character development, and that development
creates a narrative necessity: Isabel must make a
choice. The same is true of theme-suspense in
Wyndham Lewis's *Self-Condemned.* Only where we
have suspense creating a necessity, either fulfilled or
not, are we conscious of feeling suspense. This usually
occurs in connection with plot. But, even when it
derives largely from other levels of the narrative, this
type of suspense depends upon subliminal-suspense,
and the general statement then is one of potentiality.

Authors work within this potentiality. It is the
subliminal-suspense that engages us with the fictional
world, and it is subliminal-suspense to which we most
immediately react. The dynamics of those reactions
are the subject of this study.

69

II

Levels of Narration

The Varieties of Temporal Analysis

Four Levels of Narration

Narratives are always integrated. One cannot read *Moby Dick,* for example, without reading all at the same time its style, its actions, its characters, its values, and so on. Still, we often find it logically convenient to consider one level of a narrative at a time. The "approach" to, the "yearning" for, the metaphysical "*noumenon,* the rational object" behind the mystery of life,[1] is the *theme* of *Moby Dick.* This theme is embodied in a journey. The search for the rational is also one of the themes of *Miss Lonelyhearts.* Here, however, instead of a unified journey, we find a series of encounters. The difference spurs us to make comparisons between the works. We might wish to say that the experience of Melville in the 1840s is monolithic, while the experience of West in the 1920s is fragmented. *Moby Dick* explores the problem of the rational behind the irrational for a world grown up in religion,[2] while *Miss Lonelyhearts* explores that same problem for a world splintered by war and depression. The logical operation that we have performed here is relatively simple. We have

71

arbitrarily separated one level of narration, theme, from the whole work. Then we have abstracted information about that level of narration from another work. The similarity of theme alone, in the face of the obvious differences between the narratives as wholes, impels us to ask questions whose answers tell us more than we might otherwise have learned about either work. One could easily read *Moby Dick*, say, without stopping to analyze the constitution of its audience. Thus, despite the apparent violence that separation does, such separation itself is a potentially powerful tool in our critical workshop.

This particular tool lies at the heart of generic criticism. A genre is a group (a *class* in symbolic logic) defined by some common characteristic (definition). Genre criticism is useful exclusively and inclusively. Exclusive questions refer genre X to the rest of literature, or to other genres. For example, what place does genre X have in the development of literature? What is the relation of genre X to genre Y? Inclusive questions probe the composition of the genre, the relations among the elements of the class. Epic A is of genre X, and so is epic B; how does this similarity illuminate their differences? How is it that so many different epics can all be part of genre X? To couch the methods of genre criticism in algebraic notation may seem antiliterary, but it is a useful procedure because it implies the universal applicability of the method. Such an abstract formulation hints at the pervasive use we make of genre criticism. A young couple considers whether to move into either a house or an apartment. This is a generic distinction. They decide on a house. Own or rent? Another generic distinction, though this time based on financial rather than architectural considerations. They decide to rent. Then they see as many rentable houses as possible and make inclusive distinctions. The power of a generic approach comes from the possibility of selecting defining characteristics along purely theoretical lines. Critics interested in the historical development of literature, like Scholes and Kellogg in *The Nature of Narrative,* choose genres on historical grounds. Critics interested in formal analyses, like Frank in *The Widening Gyre,* choose genres on formal grounds. In our investigation, where we are interested in the temporality of narrative which creates the engagement of suspense, generic distinctions should center on those attributes of a narrative which develop through time.

Of course, since narratives are written in language, everything that takes place in a narrative takes place through time. This motivated the extreme concern with style in chapter 1. But other things, theme, for example, not only take place in time, but develop through time. What shall we do with *The Marble Faun?*[3] If we are interested in Hawthorne, our genre is immediately defined by the corpus of that author's work. But perhaps we are interested in other things. *The Marble Faun* works out a so-called international theme. And so does *The Ambassadors.* Immediately we begin to ask questions about Americanism, and to compare works separated by half a century. But then, *Self-Condemned* also works out an international theme. However, this novel stands against the other two within our genre by virtue of the fact that in this last the New World is the foreign country. And yet, in all three, the Old World is the corrupt. Perhaps we are coming closer to saying something about the entire genre defined by the international theme. We need more members of the class to test the hypothesis, but even within this small sample, we become aware that the newness of the New

World acts as an objective correlative for innocence. And so in all three, we become aware of the question of innocence and evil. The generic approach (thematic in this instance) casts light on the entire genre.

A system of genres is developed in chapter 3. Here, seeing the value of a generic approach, we must assert that, by virtue of the temporality of narrative, by virtue of our subliminal engagement through suspense, we ought to develop defining principles which make use of the developmental in narrative, for the developmental is at the heart of our reading. Thematic development is one such genre-defining principle.

Character development, thematic development, and plot all occur through time. For that reason, they are susceptible to description in the same terms that we have used for style. These four—character, theme, plot, and style—are *levels* of narration. By this term we mean to be mindful that each proceeds *through* the course of any given narrative. We often find it convenient, as with the international theme or the theme of *Moby Dick,* to consider these levels as things apart. But, as Henry James has said, "What is character but the determination of incident?" "What is incident but the illustration of character?"[4] He is, of course, correct in reminding us that the levels of narration, when we try to exhaustively analyze any work, are not ultimately separable. The interrelations among the levels are radical. But we often do not feel this, and the blurry boundary between the levels seems to disappear when we fix our attention on a single level. In discussing the "spongy tract" which is the body of English literature, E. M. Forster says:

> **Parts . . . seem more fictitious than other parts, it is true: near the middle, on a tump of grass, stand**

Miss Austen with the figure of Emma by her side, and Thackeray holding up Esmond.[5]

Emma Woodhouse and Henry Esmond have no existence outside their fictional realities, and those fictional realities, as we have seen, are constituted by the complex and interrelated effects of all levels of narration. But we do agree with Forster, somehow, and find ourselves able to discuss the characters alone. Similarly, we can, as in the first chapter, discuss style alone. Or, as Frye does in his "Theory of Mythos,"[6] discuss plot alone. Despite the fact that these levels are not actually discrete and mutually exclusive, they seem to form the most significant *loci* for both attention and discussion. Examples will make the utility of this observation clear.

One of the primary types of comparisons that we have discussed is the anticontextual. In this type of comparison, the perceived bit seems to violate the context in which it occurs. This context can be either freight which we have brought forward alone to the reading of the perceived bit or freight of which we are reminded, whose memory is revivified, by an eidetic bit preceding the perceived bit, so that the anticontextual comparison seems to be not immediately between the perceived bit and its context, but between the perceived bit and the eidetic bit. Twain's *The Man That Corrupted Hadleyburg* depends upon creating a false notion of virtue to be undercut in both action and style. In the end, the moral is that there is an educating power in sin. Such a moral itself is anticontextual, for sin is bad, while education is good. Notice how Twain uses "pride," a sin, to create this tension stylistically. The following is taken from the very beginning of the story:

It was many years ago. Hadleyburg was the most honest and upright town in all the region about. It

> had kept that reputation unsmirched during three generations, and was prouder of it than of any other of its possessions. It was so proud of it, and so anxious to insure its perpetuation, that it began to teach the principles of honest dealing to its babies in the cradle . . .[7]

"Babies in the cradle" are presumed innocent in a Christian world. They have no need to be taught honesty. That the people of Hadleyburg are "anxious" to teach these babies honesty shows that, below their outward probity, they are ever aware of the attractive force of sin. This functions anticontextually, for the context is established when the narrator says that "Hadleyburg was the most honest and upright town in all the region about." The diachronic suspense of the style of the entire piece is resolved in anticontextual comparisons, the last being the moral.

If we consider the bits to be bits of thematic information, however, instead of bits of stylistic information, we can often make the same claim for the anticontextual use of suspense in theme. Consider "Of the Millennium," by Isak Dinesen. It is reproduced in its entirety:

> At the time when the near return of Christ to the earth had become a certainty, a Committee was formed to decide upon the arrangements for His reception. After some discussion, it sent out a circular which prohibited all waving and throwing about of palm-branches as well as all cries of "Hosanna."
> When the Millennium had been going on for some time, and joy was universal, Christ one evening said to Peter that He wanted, when everything was quiet, to go out for a short walk with him alone.
> "Where do you want to go, my Lord?" Peter asked.

"I should like," answered the Lord, **"just to take
a walk from the Praetorium along that long road,
up to the Hill of Calvary."**[8]

Here the theme is quite simply the millennium. That
much is established by the title. The millennium is essentially a static concept; it is the unchanging,
beatific epoch which will follow, by the grace of God,
our current chaotic era. The idea of the otherness of
the millennium is undercut by incorporating elements
of our era into its discussion: *Committee, circular.*
The concept of the divine grace motivating the
millennium is undercut by the apparent human intervention, and the intrusion of human formalities:
become a certainty (presumably to the people of
Earth), *arrangements, reception, discussion,* human
prohibition. The time of divine peace is destroyed by
the particular type of peace decreed: no *waving and
throwing about of palm-branches* or *cries of "Hosan-
na."* Thus, in the context of the first paragraph, the
Millennium of the second paragraph is anticontextual, as also, in that silent time, is Christ's
request to go for a walk *when everything was quiet.*
Christ, the narrator implies, is aware of the way in
which the millennium is being perverted. Christ
should rule, but instead, anticontextually, he yearns
to die, *up to the Hill of Calvary.* By having Christ
himself assent to the undercutting of the millennium,
the theme actually develops from the hypothetical
coming of the millennium to the impossibility of man
making way for the millennium.

One could, of course, treat the words we have
italicized from "Of the Millennium" not as referring
to a coherent theme, but rather as words themselves,
in which case we would be doing a stylistic analysis.
However, this stylistic analysis, in the vocabulary so
far developed, would come to the same conclusion

that our thematic analysis arrived at. This agreement indicates how easily one level of narration which we try to isolate for study may slip over into another. But it would be wrong to conclude a priori that in a given narrative all levels of narration operate in the same way. In the passage from *Moby Dick* which we have examined stylistically (p. 20), the theme develops anticontextually, resulting finally in an unresolvable ambiguity, while the style, highly metaphoric, is procontextual. The possibility that theme and style may function differently in a single work is a primary motivation for accepting the apparently arbitrary distinction between the levels of narration. Some works (say *Finnegans Wake*) oblige us to concentrate on their style, while others, like our small tale from Isak Dinesen, seem to demand a thematic treatment.

Other works, of course, make similar demands for plot or character. In Martial's little piece called "On Galla," character is the main concern. The idea of the millennium in Dinesen was progressively recontextualized, undercut again and again until it had been completely reversed. Here the courtesan's character is repeatedly undercut. The anticontextual comparisons (made in harshly numerical terms) change her station completely. This piece too is reproduced in its entirety:

> Once upon a time Galla's demand was twenty thousand sesterces; and I admit she was not much too dear at the price. A year passed by: "I am yours," she said, "for ten thousand sesterces." This seemed to me more than she had asked before. Six months afterward, when she came down to two thousand, I offered one thousand, which she refused. About two or three months later, so far from refusing this sum, she herself lowered her demand to four gold pieces. I declined to give it, and

then she asked me to give her a hundred sesterces; but even this sum seemed greatly too much. A miserable sportula of a hundred farthings would then have brought us together; that is, she proposed to accept it; but I told her I had bestowed it on my slave. Could she descend lower than this? She did; she now offers herself for nothing; but I decline.[9]

Notice how the anticontextual comparisons still depend upon a clearly apprehensible structure as a framework within which to operate. The time progresses from a distant past, in ever smaller stages, to the narrative present (*Once upon a time, a year passed, six months afterward, two or three months later, then, now*). Similarly, the price drops from the astronomical, in ever smaller stages, to the inconsequential (*twenty thousand sesterces, ten thousand sesterces, two thousand, one thousand, four gold pieces, a hundred sesterces, a hundred farthings, nothing*). These accelerated diminutions are paralleled by an accelerating disparity between what Galla asks and what the narrator feels she is worth (from *I admit she was not much too dear at the price* to a flat *but I decline*). Anticontextual comparisons never really destroy the context, for if the context were destroyed, the narrative would not seem coherent. But within the established framework (even one, like Martial's, in which negation itself is the principle), the anticontextual comparisons can result from structural suspense (in this case, character-suspense).

In the same way that we have found anticontextuality dominating style, theme, and character, we can also find it dominating plot. The most obvious case is dramatic irony, where we know one thing to be true, but a character acts as if another were the case. The actions compare anticontextually. However, in drama, the actions can be presented simultaneously.

Narrative Suspense

The closest analog to dramatic irony in narrative is
the mediated character, the character who mediates
his own actions, conclusions, and so forth through his
own notions, which happen to be at odds with the
world. This is common in the case of the untrustworthy narrator, for example, Coverdale in
Blithedale Romance. There, an ostensibly procontextual style discusses ostensibly procontextually
organized actions. But the radical misinterpretations
on the part of the I-narrator make both mutually
anticontextual. This case of the untrustworthy
narrator is worth mentioning because it so common.
However, it is also quite complex.

A simpler illustration of plot alone functioning
anticontextually is Chekov's *Vanka,* a beautiful little
story of a nine-year-old orphan, Ivan (Vanka) Jukov,
writing a letter to his grandfather. Writing a letter is
primarily a mental act, and Vanka's two mental lives
(his knowledge of his horrible apprenticeship in
frightening Moscow and his idyllic memories of his
home village) create a poignant antithesis for the
reader. The story begins:

> Nine-year-old Vanka Jukov, who has been appren-
> tice to the shoemaker Aliakhine for three months,
> did not go to bed the night before Christmas. He
> waited till the master and mistress and the
> assistants had gone out to an early church service,
> to procure from his employer's cupboard a small
> phial of ink and a penholder with a rusty nib; then,
> spreading a crumpled sheet of paper in front of
> him, began to write.
>
> Before, however, deciding to make the first
> letter, he looked furtively at the door and at the
> window, glanced several times at the somber ikon
> on either side of which stretched the shelves full of
> lasts, and heaved a heart-rending sigh. The sheet

of paper was spread on a bench, and he himself was on his knees in front of it.

"Dear Grandfather Constantin Makaritch," he wrote, "I am writing you a letter. I wish you a Happy Christmas and all God's holy best. I have no father or mamenka, you are all I have."[10]

Already the world of the letter is established against the world of Vanka's apprenticeship, his poverty (he needs to steal ink) against his innocence, his isolation against his yearning for his grandfather. The ongoing structure here is not as complicated as the acceleration in Martial; it is simply the writing of a letter. But in the writing, the action, the mental acts, come into extreme conflict. The letter causes intermittent reverie, and Vanka imagines his home village:

> It is glorious weather, not a breath of wind, clear, and frosty; it is a dark night, but the whole village, its white roofs, and streaks of smoke from the chimneys, the trees silvered with hoarfrost, and the snowdrifts, you can see it all. The sky scintillates with bright twinkling stars, and the Milky Way stands out so clearly that it looks as if it had been polished and rubbed over with snow for the holidays . . . [*sic*]
> Vanka sighed, dipped his pen in the ink, and continued to write:
> "Last night I got a thrashing, the patron dragged me by my hair into the yard, belabored me with a shoemaker's stirrup, because, while I was rocking their brat in its cradle, I unfortunately fell asleep."

One could consider that the latter paragraph serves as a perceived bit which compares anti-contextually with that which precedes it. Were this a story that had a great deal of action, one might be tempted to treat these paragraphs as images and

81

relegate the anticontextuality to style. However, when there is nothing in the story but a succession of images, suddenly the progress of the images becomes the action, and one thinks of the letter writing not as an isolated act, but as the plot. In this case, the plot is worked out anticontextually.

Although the story is short, and the whole of it is worth reading, the ending alone, I believe, will make the point that the images, as they are arranged diachronically, are anticontextual as we read them, and that this in no way interferes with the simplicity of Vanka's view. Their conflict occurs in the reader.

"Come quick, dear Granpapa," continued Vanka, "I beseech you for Christ's sake take me from here. Have pity on a poor orphan, for here they all beat me, and I am frightfully hungry, and so bored that I can't tell you, I cry all the time. The other day the patron hit me on the head with a last; I fell to the ground, and only just returned to life. My life is a disaster, worse than any dog's . . . [sic] I send greetings to Aliona, to one-eyed Egor, and the coachman, and don't let anyone have my harmonium. I remain, your grandson, Ivan Jukov, dear Grandpapa, do come."

Vanka folded his sheet of paper in four, and put it into an envelope, purchased the night before for a kopeck. He thought a little, dipped the pen into the ink, and wrote the address:

"The village, to my grandfather." He then scratched his head, thought again, and added: "Constantin Makaritch." Pleased at having been able to write without disturbance, he put on his cap, and, omitting his sheepskin coat, ran out in his shirtsleeves into the street.

The shopman at the poulterer's, from whom he had inquired the night before, had told him that letters were to be put into post-boxes, and from thence they were conveyed over the whole earth in mail troikas by drunken post-boys and to the sound of bells. Vanka ran to the first post-box and slipped his precious letter into the slit.

An hour afterwards, lulled by hope, he was sleeping soundly. In his dreams he saw a stove, by the stove sat his grandfather with his legs dangling down, barefooted, and reading a letter to the cooks . . . Around the stove walks Viune wagging his tail . . .

The last image, which ends the story, is a happy one, and even a humorous one if we suppress our sympathy for Vanka, but within its context it is immensely sad. The sadness is ours, for only the reader can see both the actions of the world of postal requirements and the actions of the little boy's mind. The last thought/action operates anticontextually, for us, and we feel the sadness ourselves. The ending occurs promptly where it should in light of the larger structure, at the end of the letter. But not the end of writing. Thus, the theme too is carried out anticontextually, for, if the tale is about writing a letter, writing. Thus, the theme too is carried out anticontextually, for, if the tale is about writing a letter, the theme is brought full about, from letter-writing as salvation to letter-writing as a source of cruel hope. Character development seems irrelevant here (the whole story is but four pages). The style is procontextual, always supporting the context it treats, and thereby creating a narrative attitude which validates both the harshness of the patron and the orphan's hopes. Only we know that the two cannot be reconciled, and that it is the boy who will suffer.

It is important that, by making the distinctions among levels of narration, we can go a long way toward describing the piece under consideration. If we cast back to "gooseberries" (discussed above, pp. 26 ff.), we can see that the frame and central story there come into conflict in a way similar to that of Vanka's two mental worlds. Again we have theme and plot working anticontextually, again a procontextual style, and again no appreciable character development. Also in "Gooseberries," we see that the final affect of the story resides in the reader. Perhaps we have begun to characterize Chekov's method.

But the critical method developed so far is inadequate to making enough genre distinctions to develop a truly useful affective genre theory. Although our four levels of narration (style, theme, character, and plot) seem to include most of the immediately interesting aspects of a narrative, the neutral/procontextual/anticontextual distinction is too broad. Within it, we would find that both Gottfried's *Tristan* and Dickens's *Bleak House* are procontextual at all levels of narration. While this itself might lead us to interesting generic investigations, we can further refine the critical terms by which we describe the functioning of suspense.

Types of Comparisons

Arthur Koestler has written a brilliant psychophysiological study of what he calls *the comic,* as the first part of his *Insight and Outlook.*[11] The literary genre which he primarily investigates is the joke (and perhaps it would be better to call his theory a theory of *the joke,* rather than of *the comic*). In order to perform his analyses, he lays down a theoretical groundwork which we can easily understand, for, once we translate his terminology, we see that he arrives at many of the conclusions that we have arrived at through diachronic structural analysis. For example, we have noted how the mind skips over irrelevant associations, say associations with allusive words. Koestler calls the associative power of words and of related systems of words the *selective operator of the field* (p. 39). "... *each operative field tends to facilitate its permitted type of association and to inhibit all others*" (p. 41). Similarly, as we have noted that the primary engagement with the text is subliminal, that we cannot both read a text and concentrate on its most fundamental structure, Koestler notes that

> the selective operator (or some of its components) which coordinates and systematizes activity usually belongs to a lower level of consciousness than that activity itself (p. 45).

This is an observation important for Koestler's theory, for it creates the possibility of multiple operative fields working in the text while the reader is consciously aware of but one. In our terminology, we would say that the reader can carry forward, to the reading of any given perceived bit, numerous contexts: contexts for each of the levels of narration and even multiple contexts for an individual level of narration. For example, there are a number of interwoven plots in *Middlemarch*. Each serves as a context for bits of plot information about the separate characters. But Featherstone's death, with the possibility of distribution of wealth to almost any of the main characters, serves as a bit in each of those plot contexts. For Koestler, concerned with the joke, the possibility of multiple contexts leads him to a notion he calls *bisociation*. Bisociation is the sudden radical connection between two (or more) contexts, and it stands against *association* in the same way that paratactic styles stand against hypotactic ones.[12] He illustrates how this works in a joke taken from Bergson:

> A dignitary of Monte Carlo is much admired for the not less than thirty-six medals which he wears on his breast. Somebody asks him by what heroic deeds he earned them. "That's simple," he says, "I got a medal for my faithful service to the prince; I put it on a number at the roulette table and the number came up" (p. 19).

Koestler says that this joke has the "two basic factors of the comic [the joke]: its *logical geometry or pattern,* and its *emotional tension or charge*" (p. 20). The patterns are the lines in his diagram (below), and the tension is their disjunction:

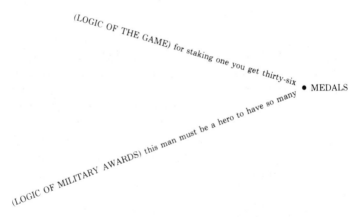

To Koestler's analysis, we should add that, although we read consciously the context of military awards, the game context is already latent because of the phenomenology of *Monte Carlo.* Additionally, in the original French, the number *thirty-six* would have been a clue that we were reading a joke, because thirty-six is the standard French number for an exaggerated amount (something like the American million: "I've asked you not to do that a million times!"). Bisociation occurs, in the diagram above, at the dot.

As Koestler treats it, the important thing about bisociation is the way it sneaks up on one: we are not consciously expecting the precise punch line, and when it comes, it creates a "back-formation" in the reader's mind which is the second line of logic. This is clearest when the second line of logic is back-formed by a single word which suddenly vivifies the second (till then latent) context.

A man about town showed his devotion to a young actress by lavish gifts. Being a respectable girl, she took the first opportunity of discouraging his attentions by telling him that her heart already belonged to another man. "I never aspired as high as that," was his polite answer (p. 32).

Here, the *as high as that,* specifically, the *high,* creates the back-formation of a second line of logic to which we must leap. Koestler claims, on the basis of physiological studies, that whereas our intellect is quite agile, our emotions are almost inert.

Our understanding does jump from the first field to the second, whereas our emotion, incapable of performing the sudden jump, is spilled (p. 60).

This "spilling" comes out as laughter.

This last joke serves well to illustrate the relation between style-suspense and theme-suspense. In a joke, the bisociation is what we are after. Anything that follows detracts from the impact of the joke, for it gives us something else to engage our consciousness. For that reason, a periodic sentence, one in which context discharges at the end, is ideal for the joke. The last line of the actress joke would be better if it read: "I never," he replied politely, "aspired that high." As we have noted above (p. 54), such periodicity is at the heart of *Tristram Shandy*. In both Sterne and the examples from Koestler, the syntax of the periodic sentence creates subliminal suspense.[13]

In discussing metaphor and irony in order to develop the notion of comparison, we treated comparisons as if the perceived bit always functioned within a single context. This, in light of the evidence of jokes, is insufficient. The impact of Koestler's bisociation depends upon the perceived bit operating within multiple contexts. Let us then reserve the term *comparison* for perceived bits operating with single eidetic bits or in single contexts (e.g., "On Galla," p. 78), *bisociation* for perceived bits operating with many eidetic bits or in multiple contexts. As we had procontextual and anticontextual comparisons, we can also have procontextual and anticontextual bisociations. Jokes make anticontextual bisociations. The oxymoron at the end of Melville's "Lee Shore" passage (p. 21) makes a procontextual bisociation. This is evident in that both parts of the oxymoron serve procontextually (metaphorically, here) within their respective contexts.

But there is a further difference between the passage from *Moby Dick* and the joke, a difference that suggests a further distinction. Bisociation, as Koestler treats it, discharges the contexts against each other. The act signals the end of the structure, and it is for that reason that the periodic sentence improves the punch line. Melville's bisociation does not destroy the diachronic potential of the twin contexts of the "Lee Shore." Something is left over and the lee shore becomes a complex symbol which we carry forward in our reading. In the same way, the post-box near the end of *Vanka* (p. 82) makes a bisociation which leaves something for us to carry forward in our reading. Indeed, another paragraph separates the

post-box from the end of the story. Such bisociations
are residual: the radical connection of the bisociation
leaves a residue which can further serve as context for
yet more perceived bits (whereas the discharging
bisociation, as in jokes, leaves only a "motionless
memory" having minimal diachronic implications).
But the bisociation of *Vanka,* unlike that of "The Lee
Shore," is anticontextual, for in Chekov one context
acts to destroy the other, whereas in Melville the two
contexts cooperate to describe two aspects of a single
phenomenon. There is a residue. We have made, then,
a series of distinctions among the ways in which the
suspense structures can function: comparison/bisocia-
tion, procontextual/anticontextual/neutral, and dis-
charge/residue.

 We have seen this last distinction operating in
bisociative structures, and we would at first assume
that we should be able to see it operating in comparative structures also. However, this is not the case.
Discharge depends upon multiple contexts, so comparative structures are necessarily limited to residual
comparisons, for, by definition, comparative structures have but one context. With this proviso, we can
use our distinctions to examine the corpus of
narrative.

Empirical Generalizations

Toward an Affective Genre Theory

The Generic Grid

We can organize the distinctions among the ways suspense operates into a grid which shows them in relation to each other:

	procontextual	anticontextual	neutral
residual / comparisons \ *discharge*	A	B	1
residual / bisociations \ *discharge*	C	D	2
	E	F	3

Fig. 1. Theoretical Generic Grid

If we assume that all levels of narration in some work operate in the manner prescribed by the parameters locating any given box of our grid, then that work will be paradigmatic for some genre defined affectively through the analysis of suspense structures. That is, if

91

our genre-defining principles depend upon diachronic analysis, we would divide all narratives into nine possible camps. The second rank is excluded by hatch marks for, as we have noted, discharging comparisons are impossible. Further, the neutral column is set apart from the rest by manner of notation because, if all levels of narration in some work functioned neutrally, we would no longer be in a rhetorical situation, and rhetoric (p. 14) is essential to narrative.

(Reflection reveals what manner of discourse is implied in the numbered boxes. In the completely neutral situation, we have the ideal language of symbolic logic. Genre 1, then, includes propositional statements; genre 2, enthymemes; and genre 3, syllogisms. This, however, is not important for the study of narrative. It is merely necessary to note that the numbered genres are not part of the corpus of narratives that we study.)

Thus, we find ourselves with six lettered genres theoretically established as a framework for the discussion of narrative. This seems, in light of the traditional proliferation of generic distinctions, a singularly small number. However, the number of distinctions possible is a direct function of the genre-defining principles which we choose, and says nothing about what authors must do. These six categories are not prescriptions, but descriptions. Further, in terms of suspense these make only exclusive distinctions. Analysis will show the value of making at least one further inclusive distinction in order to bring this scheme more into line with traditional categories. Let us proceed to the analyses.

The Folk Tale
Vladimir Propp has done extensive diachronic analysis of a genre whose English translation is "folk

tale."[1] (Propp's translator, Laurence Scott, suggests
that perhaps "fairy tale" would be more apt since so
many of the tales considered concern heroes and
magic. This thematic concern is worth noting, but
does not alter a structural analysis.) Propp's conclusions, even though based on a highly restricted corpus, are startling. Basically, Propp divides a tale into
actions; these are roughly equivalent to the *gross con-
stituent units* that Lévi-Strauss uses for his synchronic analyses of myth.[2] An action is what one personage (even a magical object) does to another. Thus,
the notion of action combines the levels of plot and
theme. This combination seems extremely useful in a
genre characterized by neutral style and the virtual
absence of character development. The following folk
tale from the *Afanas'ev Collection* is the one that
Propp treats in detail. The parenthetical passages are
Propp's reductions (pp. 96-98).

> There lived an old man and an old woman; they had
> a daughter and a little son. "Daughter, daughter,"
> said the mother, "we are going out to work and we
> will bring you back a little bun, sew you a little
> dress and buy you a little kerchief. Be wise, take
> care of your little brother, and do not leave the
> courtyard." The elders went away, and the
> daughter forgot what they had ordered her to do.
> She placed her little brother on the grass under a
> window and ran out into the street and became ab-
> sorbed in playing and having fun.
>   The swan-geese flew down, seized the little boy
> and carried him away on their wings.
>   The little girl came back, looked, but her brother
> wasn't there. She gasped and rushed hither and
> thither, but he wasn't anywhere. She called out;
> she burst into tears, wailing that harm would come
> to her from her father and mother, but her little
> brother did not answer. She ran out into the open

field; the swan-geese sped away into the distance and disappeared beyond the dark wood. The swan-geese had long before acquired an ill fame, caused much mischief, and had stolen many a little child. The girl guessed that they had carried off her little brother, and she set out to catch up with them. She ran and ran until she came upon a stove.

"Stove, stove, tell me: where have the geese flown?"

"If you eat my little rye-cake, I'll tell." "Oh, we don't even eat cakes made of wheat in my father's house." (A meeting with an apple tree and a river follows. Similar proposals and similar insolent replies.)

She would have run through the fields and wandered in the forest a long time if she had not by good fortune met a hedgehog. She wished to nudge him, but was afraid of pricking herself. "Little hedgehog, little hedgehog," she asked, "did you not see where the geese have flown?" "Away, over there," he pointed.

She ran and came upon a hut on chicken legs. It was standing and turning around.

In the hut sat Baba Jaga, hag-faced and with a leg of clay. The little brother also sat there on a little bench, playing with golden apples.

His sister saw him, stole up, seized him and carried him away, and the geese flew after her in pursuit; the evil-doers were overtaking them; where was there to hide?

(Once again a triple testing by the same characters, but with positive answer which evokes the aid of the tester himself in the form of rescue from pursuit. The river, the apple tree, and the stove hide the little girl. The tale ends with the little girl's arrival home.)

The most immediately striking structural principle here is the principle of threeness. Tests come in three's, answers come in three's, and most of the sentences are tripartite: "[1] we will bring you back a little bun, [2] sew you a little dress and [3] buy you a little kerchief. [1] Be wise, [2] take care of your little brother, and [3] do not leave the courtyard." This threeness, however, is a cultural, not a strictly narrative, phenomenon. We shall take it up below.

Propp, analyzing the folk tale by actions, notices something which is even more remarkable, that the general statement of the actions in this folk tale is identical to the general statement of the actions in every folk tale. To be more precise, there are (Propp concludes) thirty-one possible actions. Of these, some are obligatory, others optional. However, regardless of the number of optional actions a tale may contain, the order of those actions which are included is always the same. This is to say that a folk tale is like a string of thirty-one numbered beads, each bead representing an action. Propp finds that some actions, if they occur, must always be followed directly by a second action (say, question and response), and so they come in pairs. Let us say that the obligatory actions are 1 and 2, 7 and 8, 23 and 24, and 31. Then, in any given folk tale, say one which also includes actions 5, 11, and 26, the order of those actions as we actually find them collected by folklorists will be 1, 2, 5, 7, 8, 11, 23, 24, 26, 31. Although some beads on the string may not be present, the order of the remaining beads is always the same.

Propp provides the general statements for each action. The following is the first obligatory one:

**One of the Members of a Family
Absents Himself from Home.**
   1. *The person absenting himself can be a member of the older generation.* **Parents leave for work (113).**

95

> "The prince had to go on a distant journey, leaving his wife to the care of strangers" (265). "Once, he (a merchant) went away to foreign lands" (197). Usual forms of absentation: going to work, to the forest, to trade, to war, "on business."
> 2. *An intensified form of absentation is represented by the death of parents.*
> 3. *Sometimes members of the younger generation absent themselves.* They go visiting (101), fishing (108), for a walk (137), out to gather berries (244).

The numbers in parentheses refer to the tales in the *Afanas'ev Collection* of more than four hundred Russian folk tales. Propp's method was really quite simple. He analyzed the actions of every tale in the collection. He claims that all thirty-one actions had occurred by the time he had gone through the first ten narratives. The remainder of the collection merely validated his tentative conclusions and gave him the insight into the necessity behind the ordering of the actions. He then took these conclusions and tested them against the more than twelve hundred folk tales in the international *Aarne-Thompson Collection* (the more complete *Stith Thompson Index* was not available in Propp's lifetime). Astoundingly, the conclusions bore the weight of this test. The data thus far presented are what led Propp to his final conclusion: *"All fairy* [folk] *tales are of one type in regard to their* [diachronic] *structure"* (p. 23).

The motive for inserting *diachronic* before *structure* grows out of an understanding of Propp's method. His unit of analysis is the *action,* and an action is a temporal unit, a structure in time. Thus, his investigation of the ordering of actions is in fact an investigation of diachronic structures (a point which Propp himself makes clear in the introduction to *The Morphology of the Folktale*). That is, Propp has been studying suspense. In our terminology we would want to note that the folk tale structure is comparative (rather than bisociative): each action (combined levels of theme and plot) operates in the single context of all that came before it. Further, these comparisons are always procontextual, for the basic theme and plot of the folk tale are never undercut by any of the individual perceived bits (actions). And last, these procontextual comparisons are always residual. On the one hand, they must be, for discharging comparisons are impossible theoretically. But on the other hand, it is empirically true that each action only serves to add to the context which then carries forward. In fact, the context carries forward so powerfully that folk tales are used to teach cultural norms.

As the example makes clear, the levels of character and style function neutrally in folk tales. Thus, we can say that all operative levels of the narrative function according to the parameters of box A (p. 91) and that the body of narratives that we call folk tale are part of genre A. This description still seems valid when applied to folk tales Propp did not consider, for example, the Pawnee folk tale called "The Ghost Wife":

> One time there were living together a man and his wife. They had a young child. The woman died. The man was very sad, and mourned for his wife.
> One night he took the child in his arms, and went out from the village to the place where his wife was buried, and stood over the grave, and mourned for his wife. The little child was very helpless, and cried all the time. The man's heart was sick with grief and loneliness. Late in the night he fell asleep, fainting and worn out with sorrow. After a while he awoke, and when he looked up, there was the one who had died. She spoke to her husband, and said,

"You are very unhappy here. There is a place to go where we would not be unhappy. Where I have been nothing bad happens to one. Here, you never know what evil will come to you. You and the child had better come to me."

The man did not want to die. He said to her, "No; it will be better if you can come back to us. We love you. If you were with us we would be unhappy no longer."

For a long time they discussed this, to decide which one should go to the other. At length the man by his persuasions overcame her, and the woman agreed to come back. She said to the man, "If I am to come back you must do exactly as I tell you for four nights. For four days the curtain must remain let down before my sleeping place; it must not be raised; no one must look behind it."

The man did as he had been told, and after four days had passed, the curtain was lifted, and the woman came out from behind it. Then they all saw her, first her relations, and afterwards the whole tribe. Her husband and her child were very glad, and they lived happily together.

A long time after this, the man took another wife. The first wife was always pleasant and good-natured, but the new one was bad-tempered, and after some time she grew jealous of the first woman, and quarreled with her. At length, one day the last married became angry with the other, and called her bad names, and finally said to her, "You ought not to be here. You are nothing but a ghost, anyway."

That night when the man went to bed, he lay down, as was his custom, by the side of his first wife. During the night he awoke, and found that his wife had disappeared. She was seen no more. The next night after this happened, the man and the child both died in sleep. The wife had called them to her. They had gone to that place where there is a

living. [In Pawnee English of the period, *living* means the security of a livelihood and does not stand against *dying.*]

This convinced everybody that there is a hereafter.[3]

Propp's conclusions are as valid for "The Ghost Wife" as for the Baba Jaga tale. Familiarity with *The Morphology of the Folktale* would make this apparent in detail. Here, let it suffice to note some of the grosser structural similarities. Both folk tales begin with a spare scene-setting element (an alpha-element in Propp's terminology). Both proceed to the obligatory absentation. Both absentations cause difficulties for the main characters. Both main characters leave their homes. Both encounter magic. Both seem to have achieved the object of their quest (finding the brother and the return of the wife). Both have difficulty once the object is apparently gained (pursuit by the swan-geese, scolding by the second wife). Both achieve a return to security. I do not know how Afanas'ev elicited his tales from the Russian peasantry, but I can easily picture a mother telling the Baba Jaga tale to her daughter and concluding with: "And so little daughters should always mind their parents." This moral, certainly implicit in the story, would then parallel structurally the last sentence of "The Ghost Wife." Both belong in genre A. This leads to our first empirical generalization: Genre A contains folk tales.

Having these two structurally similar narratives before us, it is easy to see that the question of threeness is not a strictly narrative phenomenon. In western culture, as has so often been noted, all things tend to come in three's: the Trinity, the three ages of man, three-on-a-match, Hegelian philosophy. But the widespread prevalence of threeness indicates a learned trait, not some necessary part of man's mental equipment. As Ruth Benedict points out in discussing the Zuni Indians of the American Southwest,[4] fourness is as integral a part of Amerindian culture as threeness is of western culture. The *four days* and *four nights* stand out glaringly in the unadorned Pawnee tale. Even some of the sentences are quadripartite. "[1] One night he took the child in his arms, and [2] went out from the village to the place where his wife was buried, and [3] stood over the grave, and [4] mourned for his wife." There is no such sentence in the Russian tale. By virtue of the beautiful simplicity that folk tales have, by virtue of their single context, they become ideal vehicles for incorporating elements of the cultures which produce them, even while they show a cross-cultural generic similarity.

However, it would be wrong to conclude on the evidence of folk tales that all members of genre A are "simple." Folk tales actually operate on two levels of narration only. Also, they engage the reader (listener) primarily with a single character. It is possible to find a work that fulfills the parameters of genre A in all levels of narration.

The Epic

The traditional genre which most nearly gives us works that fall within genre A and operate rhetorically at all levels of narration is the epic. The members of this genre, and the Homeric examples especially, are clearly complex works. However, one can profitably treat them as forming a polar possibility with folk tale in defining a range of works for genre A. As Northrop Frye points out in his essay on "Specific Encyclopaedic Forms,"[5] an epic is the "inclusive manifestation of the workings of a principle." It is important that for each epic there is *one* principle. This is the structural point that emerges from Albert B. Lord's milestone, *The Singer of Tales*.[6] The folk tale is simple, operating rhetorically only on the levels of theme and action; its primary concern is with the individual, for whom the culture is assumed paratactically. The epic is much more complex. It operates rhetorically on the levels of theme, plot, character, and style; the concern is the large one of society, for which the hero's role is assumed paratactically.

Despite this large social concern, and despite the epic's complexity, a given epic may truly operate within a single context. Through his study of modern-day Yugoslav oral epicists, Lord arrived at the notion that the composition of epics was impossible without the existence in the culture of a large pool of formulaic expressions and actions upon which the poet may draw.[7]

Formulas, and groups of formulas, both large and small, serve only one purpose. They provide a means for telling a story in song and verse. The tale's the thing.[8]

That is, an epic makes us ask, "and then?"

In many epics, the "tale" and the culture are radically united, and the story of the nation becomes the single context within which all the formulae operate procontextually. In Vergil, for example, that context is the foundation of Rome. The

poem is an integrated whole in which each incident, no matter what its source, has its bearing on the poet's theme, the destined establishment of Roman power in Italy.[9]

Vergil saw his *Aeneid* as operating within a long generic tradition of epic. He defined this tradition in terms of certain static qualities: the high style, the machinery of the gods, the hero, the grand theme, and so forth. Yet, despite these static conceptions, he produced a work whose diachronic structure uses a suspense similar not only to that in folk tale, but to the suspense in Homer.[10]

> Arms, and the man I sing, who, forced by Fate,
> And haughty Juno's unrelenting hate,
> Expelled and exiled, left the Trojan shore.
> Long labours, both by sea and land, he bore,
> And in the doubtful war, before he won
> The Latin realm, and built the destined town;
> His banished gods restored to rites divine;
> And settled sure succession in his line,
> From whence the race of Alban fathers come,
> And the long glories of majestic Rome[11]

These lines tell the reader what to wait for.

Vergil's opening is still the most powerful single statement of the work's theme. Notice, however, that already in this statement we have suspense structures which fulfill the requirements of genre A. The style is metaphorical (banished *gods,* long labours *bore*), procontextual in a way that leaves a strong residue (*Fate, restored, succession, fathers, long* glories). Aeneas's character, to the extent that one can say it develops, develops always in accord with his unchanging destiny (he is frequently commanded directly by the gods). The plot, of course, is bent entirely to the realization of the single theme. The work ends not in Vergil's own time, but in a past just about to change into the epoch of Roman ascendency. The last bit of plot is "the death of Turnus, which removes the last barrier to the fulfillment of Rome's destiny."[12] This has a strong residual effect, and must have had an even stronger effect on the Augustan audience. It was the emperor himself, of course, who commissioned the poem as a nationalistic effort. The finished work, like the moralizing of the folk tale, has an educating potential which comes from its structure. At all levels the use of suspense is procontextual, comparative, and residual.

Vergil sets the scene for his work so as to endorse a particular culture. This is the function of the alpha-element of the folk tale. Aeneas's absentation follows the alpha-element directly in the same way that the I-action of obligatory absentation follows it in Propp's analysis of the folk tale. Even historically considered, folk tale and epic are close together. Both grow out of the culture in a very direct way; both descend from an oral tradition. What is most important from the standpoint of suspense is that these common origins happen to be expressed in similar structures, structures which are theoretically defined by the parameters of genre A. Thus, genre A contains works which fall within a range from the folk tale (individual) to the epic (social).

The distinction between emphases (individual/social) is not, though, a structural one. It is raised in order to clarify the relation between traditional categories (folk tale and epic) and our categories based on an analysis of the suspense structure (genre A). Since suspense is basic to reading a narrative, one would expect that the intuitive classifications of readers would in large measure conform to our categories. This is the case. However, many of the traditional classifications are based on sophisticated concepts which do not directly relate to diachronic structure. Thus, in *The Iliad,* surely an epic as traditionally defined, we clearly have two parallel plots. The suspense of each plot works according to the parameters of genre A, but the existence of the second plot would force us to exclude *The Iliad* as a paradigmatic example of genre A. The subject of mixing genres will be taken up in chapter 4. Here, let us note that epic *as a structural generalization* still has much in common with epic *as a traditional classification,* some traditional epics (like the *Aeneid*) actually conforming to the structural definition. Our enterprise is not only to explore the works which fulfill the theoretical parameters, but, by importing traditional terms which as closely as possible incorporate the notions of these theoretical categories, indicate the application of our genres to the study of works which have already been classified.

In the case of our genre A, we begin with the notions of comparison, procontextuality, and residue. We find that folk tales, by virtue of their structure, fall within the genre. We also find that epics, to some extent, but still by virtue of their structure (and not by virtue of their traditional definition) also fall within the genre. Since the genre is defined by principles of suspense we can then find not only structural similarities, but similarities that come from the implications of such a structure. In the case of genre A, that effect is to enforce cultural norms.

The power for educating in works of this genre comes from the necessary subliminal acceptance of the single context. If we are to read a work, the culture that lies behind it must be accepted. But in works of genre A, the culture behind the work is not far behind at all. In fact, it is so close to the surface of the work that we are even forced to treat consciously the problems of the text in the terms that that culture provides. It is this same cultural acceptance which creates the suspense that draws us through.

The Picaresque

The power and simplicity of employing a single context does not, however, imply the necessity of treating the levels of narration procontextually. The following is a complete chapter from the anonymous Spanish work, *Lazarillo de Tormes:*

> I looked for a fourth master and found one in the person of a friar of the Order of Grace. My friends the spinning women helped me make the arrangements. They said he was a relative of theirs. He had no love for choirs or meals at the monastery. His principal passion was to gad about, and he greatly enjoyed secular affairs and seeing people on all sorts of business—so much so, indeed, that he wore out more shoes than anyone else at the monastery. He gave me the first pair of shoes I ever wore out in all my life. They lasted me exactly one week. But I could not have stood trotting about after him for a longer period. For this reason and because of some other little things I leave in the inkpot, I went my way.[13]

Here the style is ironic, rather than metaphoric (*rosy-fingered dawn* or *house on chicken legs*). One expects, from the context, which is the story of Lazarillo's attempt to come up in the world, "He gave me the first pair of shoes I ever wore in my life." Instead, it is "the first pair of shoes I ever wore *out* in my life." This anticontextual style is present phenomenologically for those familiar with the Renaissance audience. For Lazarillo, *master* means happiness, protection, and security; it is a benevolent term. The popular tradition of anticlericalism (which English audiences find so strongly in Chaucer) was already established when *Lazarillo* was written, so that *friar* operates anticontextually when it comes after *master*.[14] If we know this, then calling the spinning women, who arranged for Lazarillo's meeting with the friar, *friends* is also anticontextual. If we do not know this, then we still notice the anticontextuality of both style and theme when, in the next sentence, the "master" is described as the least regular and most secular monk possible.

Lazarillo is episodic. Each chapter tells of the central experience with each master. As this chapter begins with "I looked for a fourth master," the next chapter begins with "My fifth master happened to be . . ." (p. 75). Each episode is a miniature, structurally, of the entire plot. Lazarillo looks forward to his security when he meets a new master, but that security is always undercut. Similarly, the progress of the entire work ends abruptly when, instead of finally finding a good master, Lazarillo takes a wife, that is, becomes a master himself. He is secure because, due to the favor of the Archpriest of San Salvador toward Lazarillo's wife, Lazarillo gets a permanent government job. The final irony is that his continued enjoyment of this position depends upon his unwillingness to realize that the Archpriest is sleeping with his wife, thus undercutting even the marriage relationship.

On the level of character development, this unwillingness is significant. In each of the episodes, the one constant factor of Lazarillo's character, and of his narrative tone, is that he can see ironically through the pretensions of the people he meets. Thus, his acceptance of the permanent position of cuckold turns the last irony against him. Therefore, on the level of character, as well as on the levels of theme, style, and plot, *Lazarillo de Tormes* is worked out anti-contextually. Since this occurs within the single context of the main character's search for a livelihood within his society, *Lazarillo* would fall into our genre B.

Lazarillo is normally considered to be a paradigmatic example of the picaresque. Picaresque, like epic, is usually defined in terms of static qualities: the ironic *picaro* as hero and narrator, the episodic structure, the irreverence. However, these static qualities are clearly the "motionless" manifestations of diachronic narrative principles, namely anticontextual comparison. Thus, we can generalize and say that picaresque works belong to genre B.

This generalization, like the one we made with epic, is a generalization on structural grounds. Some works which have been labeled picaresque, like *Huckleberry Finn,* clearly do not fall in genre B. Twain's work has multiple contexts, and from the standpoint of suspense we would want to distinguish it from *Lazarillo.* It is aligned with it because its hero is a scalliwag and can therefore be confused with a picaro. Some readers see the plot as episodic (despite the interconnectedness of the episodes). But these notions are static and do not refer, as we intend the term *picaresque* to refer, to dynamic qualities of the reading. We import the term *picaresque,* then, for two reasons: First, the intuitive traditional groupings help indicate which works are like *Lazarillo,* and therefore share its structure. Second, the use of this term affords us the opportunity to stipulate a definition which is somewhat more precise than traditional usage, and therefore (not *only* by, but *especially* by excluding *Huckleberry Finn*) extends the usefulness of the term as an analytic concept. *Picaresque,* then, which happens traditionally to be associated with *Lazarillo,* is intended to refer to a structure, the kind of suspense structure we find in works of genre B.

These works are quite properly seen as related to the folk tale. Picaresque literature grows from an oral tradition in much the same way that folk tales do. Both assume the culture; the folk tale to validate it, the picaresque to chide it. But only gently, for, like the folk tale, the emphasis in the picaresque is on the individual. We should find then a body of works in genre B whose emphasis is on the society, in the same way that we found the relation of epic to folk tale.

The Satire

In the epic, the narrator is able to concentrate our attention on the society by having us assume the role of the hero within that society. This is accomplished in the epic by using heroes whose social roles are known to the audience before they hear the epic: Achilles, Odysseus, Aeneas. In Joel Barlow's attempt to produce an American epic, *The Columbiad* (publ. 1807), the main character is again previously known: Columbus. It is this knowledge shared by narrator and audience that allows the cultural emphasis. The residual effects in works of genre A tend to support their contexts. Barlow's purpose was

> **to inculcate the love of national liberty, and to discountenance the deleterious passion for violence and war; to show that on the basis of republican principle all good morals, as well as good government and hopes of permanent peace, must be founded.**[15]

Standing against the hero's role in society is the role of the clown.[16] The clown would be used to make us take love of national liberty as overblown chauvinism, or war as stupidity. Clowns, or clownish figures, occur in works of genre B, which is defined by the principle of anticontextuality.

Perhaps the most famous clown in literature is Till Eulenspiegel. Literally, *Eulen-spiegel* means owl-mirror, or, perhaps symbolically, wise-reflector. Eulenspiegel reflects ironically, wisely on his society. Tradition has it that Till really lived, born in Germany about 1300.[17] However, he does not appear in printed literature until 1510, so that when he does appear, he is already well established as a clown for his audience. *Eulenspiegel* is translated as *Howleglas* in the first English version (1528?). The following, "How Howleglas won the king's fool of Casimir of Poland with a great point of foolishness," is the sixteenth chapter of that English edition:

> The king of Casimir he had with him a certain fool, which fool could play upon the fiddle, wherefore the king loved him much and set great price by him. Also the king heard oftentimes tell of Howleglas, but he never could see him. And on a time it fortuned that Howleglas came into the king's palace for to ask dwelling, whereof when the king wist that Howleglas was come there to dwell, he was very glad thereof, and took him in, and made him goodly cheer.
>
> So it fortuned that the king's fool and Howleglas could not agree, and that spied the king well and thought in his mind: "What shall I do?" And then he made them both to be brought before him in the hall, and then he said to them: "Which of you two can the most foolishness? And [if] one of you do that the other will not do, I shall give him new clothing and 20 ducats. And let it be done in my presence before me and all my lords in this hall."
>
> And then they answered both to the king that they would prepare them, and within a while they came before the king and his lords. And then they began to do many proper conceits and merry touches of foolishness, one to the other, whereat the king and his lords had good laughter and good pastime thereat for to see how the one labored for to overcome the other and to win the new clothes and the 20 ducats.
>
> Then thought Howleglas: "This is good for me." Then he thought in his mind how he might do a thing that the other fool would not do. And then

came he before the king and his lords, and before them all he did shite a great turd. And when he had done so, he took a spoon and divided it in the midst [middle] with the spoon. And when he had done so, he came to the king's fool and said: "Do thou as I have done. Shite here in the midst, and when that ye have done, divide it in the midst, and take the spoon and take the one half of my turd and eat it, and I shall take the other half of thy turd and eat it."

Then answered the king's fool: "Yet had I lever [rather] than I would eat half thy turd or yet mine own, I had lever all the days of my life go naked." Then gave the king and all the lords the mastery to Howleglas, and they gave to him the new clothes and the 20 ducats. Then took he his leave and thanked the king and so departed he from thence.[18]

Here, as in *Lazarillo de Tormes,* the style is anticontextual. In the penultimate paragraph, after Howleglas defecated, he "divided it in the midst," setting up *midst* as the middle of the turd. This association is then used to deflate the court. " 'Shite here in the midst [of the lords], and when that ye have done, divide it in the midst.' " Although the style, again like *Lazarillo,* is predominantly neutral, when it is rhetorical, it operates on this principle of anticontextuality. The two jesters performed "many proper conceits." The "merry *touches* of foolishness" made the endeavor in which they *"labored."*

The theme, too, is anticontextual. Howleglas wins the favor of the court by doing the most uncourtly thing imaginable. However, whereas in the picaresque the emphasis is on the individual, here it is on the society. The noble setting is all important. Note that Howleglas is never referred to as *fool,* and he stands against the "king's fool," who is otherwise nameless. Howleglas is the common man's fool, the clown, deflating society, as Lazarillo is society's fool, easing the common man's own plight with his world.

The plot is episodic in much the same way that picaresque plots are episodic. This grows out of the anticontextual treatment of a single context. We can get but one laugh per situation, and then the story needs to move on. (N.B.: episodic structures in which there is no necessary connection among the episodes should not be confused with scenic or cinematic structures in which there is a radical connection among the apparently discrete plot elements, as in *Huckleberry Finn*.) It is not surprising then that we find each episode a structural miniature of the whole work in the same way that we did with *Lazarillo*. *Howleglas* is the story of the hero's lifetime of mockery. It ends, appropriately, with his death. But his death, like Lazarillo's marriage, is a special one that contains final ironies, this time directed against the society. Howleglas, by offering a priest the contents of an iron-bound chest, arranges to be given Extreme Unction despite his sins. When the priest reaches into the chest for his payment, he withdraws his hand besmirched with excrement. Howleglas does die, and, because he has left the contents of yet another chest to three separate parties, he is laid in state in the church. But the rats, who have developed a taste for dead flesh, disturb the coffin and give it the appearance of life. This frightens all concerned, and they run out. In order to bury the body, though, they need the money presumed to be in the chest. Each opens it in turn and finds it filled with stones. Each accuses the other of removing the money first. Finally they realize that Howleglas had not actually left them money, so in anger they decide to bury him under the gallows, a burial at public expense. As the coffin is being lowered by two ropes, the one at our hero's feet breaks, landing the coffin bolt upright in the grave. The common people see this and take it as a sign of the continuing wondrousness of the man. They throw in the dirt immediately so that for all time Howleglas remains on his feet, like any living man. Thus, even his death operates anticontextually, and the larger structure of the story of Howleglas's life stands as a continuing mockery of the expectations of society.

At this point, however, our discussion has turned from plot back to theme. The inclusion of some magical/godly intervention in the final scene is interesting for two reasons: first, it stands anticontextually against Howleglas's consistent practice of witty mockery; second, it reminds us that this member of genre B is not too distantly related to the equally simple members of genre A. *Howleglas,* like the folk tale and the epic, and like the origins of the picaresque, is a manifestation of the folk culture. Genre A contains a range of works that go from the emphasis on the individual (folk tale) to the emphasis on the society (epic); genre B contains a similar range, going from the picaresque to *Howleglas.* But what type of thing is *Howleglas?*

We have, of course, defined it already in terms of our structural parameters. But *Howleglas* has not been ignored by previous criticism. The individual episodes are usually referred to as *jests.*[19] This term, however, is bound by its necessary notion of length: all jests are short. For this reason, *jest* is not a useful generic term if we intend to keep defining our genres structurally. There is nothing in our statement of the parameters that predetermines shortness. On the other hand, the whole work *Howleglas* is usually called a satire.[20] There is good justification for this. The notion of satire always seems to carry with it the poking of fun at society. In addition, *Howleglas* is

strikingly like those works which we traditionally call
satire.

Consider the following passage from *Gulliver's
Travels.* Gulliver is asleep near the court of Lilliput:

> I was alarmed at midnight with the cries of many
> hundred people at my door; by which being sudden-
> ly awaked, I was in some kind of terror. I heard the
> word *burglum* repeated incessantly: several of the
> Emperor's court, making their way through the
> crowd, intreated me to come immediately to the
> palace, where her Imperial Majesty's apartment
> was on fire, by the carelessness of a maid of
> honour, who fell asleep while she was reading a
> romance. I got up in an instant; and orders being
> given to clear the way before me, and it being
> likewise a moonshine night, I made a shift to get to
> the palace without trampling on any of the people. I
> found they had already applied ladders to the walls
> of the apartment, and were well provided with
> buckets, but the water was at some distance. These
> buckets were about the size of a large thimble, and
> the poor people supplied me with them as fast as
> they could; but the flame was so violent that they
> did little good. I might easily have stifled it with my
> coat, which I unfortunately left behind me for
> haste, and came away only in my leathern jerkin.
> The case seemed wholly desperate and deplorable,
> and this magnificant palace would have infallibly
> been burnt down to the ground, if, by a presence of
> mind, unusual to me, I had not suddenly thought of
> an expedient. I had the evening before drank plen-
> tifully of a most delicious wine, called *glimigrim*
> (the Blefuscudians call it *flunec,* but ours is es-
> teemed the better sort), which is very diuretic. By
> the luckiest chance in the world, I had not dis-
> charged myself of any part of it. The heat I had con-
> tracted by coming very near the flames, and by my
> labouring to quench them, made the wine begin to

> operate by urine; which I voided in such a quantity,
> and applied so well to the proper places, that in
> three minutes the fire was wholly extinguished,
> and the rest of that noble pile, which had cost so
> many ages in erecting preserved from destruc-
> tion.[21]

When Howleglas relieves himself before the king,
we know it is anticontextual because of our knowledge
of kings. Swift, however, does not leave this point un-
articulated. ". . . it is capital [offense] in any person,
of what quality soever, to make water within the
precincts of the palace." But as Howleglas receives his
new clothes and twenty ducats, Gulliver is awarded a
pardon and the commendation of the king. It is only
minor (and anticontextual) that the Empress refuses
ever to use the "saved" facilities again.

Gulliver's Travels clearly belongs within genre B.
Each book sets up a single context. In Lilliput, the
context is that of the miniature court. The plot, as in
the episode above, proceeds anticontextually. The
style and the theme, due to the famous exaggerated
smallness of things, also are treated anticontextually.
"These buckets were about the size of a large
thimble." (Even the adjective *large* serves ironically
here, for thimbles, though they come in various sizes,
can never be large.) The fire is started "by the
carelessness of a maid of *honour.*" Even the I-
narrator's character development is anticontextual:
"by a presence of mind, unusual to me . . ." There
are, of course, many other points to be made about
this rich passage. The falling "asleep while reading a
romance" undercuts the notion of suspenseful engagement which the eighteenth century felt caused the
pathological addiction of maids to novels. The
digressive parenthesis on *flunec* operates anticontextually on the level of style when it shows the

narrator's attention wandering from the imminent danger. (Such digression is characteristic of Swift; he titles every other chapter of *A Tale of a Tub* as a digression.) But these considerations, though demanded by an exhaustive analysis of the passage, only help to demonstrate that *Gulliver* does belong to genre B.

Swift is perhaps the central satirist in modern literature. If his works belong in genre B, and *Howleglas* (paradigmatic for genre B) follows the same structural parameters, then we should say that satire (as defined by its suspense structure) falls within genre B. Thus, as in genre A, genre B contains a range of works, here from the picaresque to the satire. In such a scheme, satire would occupy a place in genre B analogous to that occupied by epic in genre A. Historically, of course, we find that, in the age in which satire flourished, the so-called Neoclassical period, many of the best satires were thought of as mock epics (e.g., *Mac Flecknoe*). As our model makes clear, the primary structural difference between epic and satire is that the material the former treats procontextually (metaphor), the latter treats anticontextually (irony).[22]

The Romance

Having discussed the ranges of works that fall within genre A and genre B, we have merely begun to explore the structural possibilities that exist in narrative. All of our examples show comparison; we have left unexplored the richness of bisociation. Let us begin again with the case of procontextual treatment resulting in residue, genre C in our table.

Daphnis and Chloe[23] is the story of the fated love between the title characters. From the outset, the phenomenological structure tells us that Daphnis and

Chloe are different from the people around them, and like each other. When the abandoned infant Daphnis is found by Lamon, a shepherd who becomes his foster father, the baby is

> . . . **better dressed than foundlings usually are, for it [the baby] had a little cloak dyed with genuine purple, a golden brooch, and a dagger with an ivory hilt (p. 20).**

Here we have both character development and style working procontextually, for the tokens found with Daphnis are metaphors. These metaphors, though they operate to complete the suspense structure of the paragraph of Lamon's discovery, have a residue which carries forward importantly: we know already that Daphnis is of noble birth, has a strange history yet to be revealed, and is destined for special things. The same residual procontextuality dominates Chloe's entrance. She too is found by a shepherd (this one named Dryas); she is found in the same neighborhood; she enters two paragraphs further in the narrative, and two years later in narrative time,

> . . . **and like the other it [the second baby] had tokens lying beside it—a girdle woven with gold thread, a pair of gilded sandals, and some anklets of solid gold (p. 21).**

Thus, Longus has established from the first a series of cooperating contexts: Daphnis' character development and Chloe's character development, the actions of the narrative present and the actions of the narrative history, the shepherd world and the noble world. To these are later added love as fated by the gods (Cupid and the Nymphs) and love as sexuality (taught to Daphnis by Chloe's rival, Lycaenion); the realm of the peaceful (both shepherds and nobles) and the world of the chaotic (pirates). These contexts bisociate through their effects on the main characters. But from the first we know how the apparent conflict among these contexts will work itself out. "These children grew up very quickly and were noticeably better-looking than ordinary country people" (p. 22). The contexts will cooperate toward the success of the central pair. Even as children, "While they were playing like this, Love made something serious flare up" (p. 24). Thus, each of the procontextual bisociations leaves a residue which we know will be carried forward in the story.

The character and style are clearly procontextual. So is the plot. The awaited revelation of true origins toward the end of the narrative makes all things possible. It provides for the reconciliation of the pirates with society, the financial advantage of the protagonists' foster parents, the love match between Daphnis and Chloe, the establishment of closer relations between the noble and peasant worlds, and the supremacy of Love.

It would seem that everything is thus neatly taken care of, and that the residuality of the narrative ends explosively with the last revelation. But this is not so, for the story goes on. Each of the several contexts is revivified in the last two pages and stands in a metaphoric relation to our heroes' marriage. One can notice this even in the last two paragraphs.

> **They also decorated the cave [where Chloe had been found] and set up images in it, and consecrated an altar to Love the Shepherd, and gave Pan a temple to live in instead of the pine, calling him Pan the Warrior.**
>
> **But it was only later that they did these things and invented these names. Now, when night fell, all the guests escorted them to the bridal chamber, some holding up great torches. When they were**

117

> near the door, the peasants began to sing in harsh grating voices as if they were breaking the soil with hoes instead of singing a wedding-song. But Daphnis and Chloe lay down naked together, and began to embrace and kiss one another; and for all the sleep they got that night they might as well have been owls. For Daphnis did some of the things that Lycaenion had taught him; and then for the first time Chloe realized that what had taken place on the edge of the wood had been nothing but childish play (p. 121).

In these paragraphs we have the clear bisociation of the spiritual and physical contexts for love. But the bisociation leaves a powerful residue because of the implicit image-structures. The peasants, who sing metaphorically like hoes, are singing like hoes "breaking the soil." This is Daphnis and Chloe's "first time." They had previously been "on the *edge* of the wood," and Chloe nothing but a child. Before them, then, is the growth and harvest, the succeeding times, the whole dark realm of the wood, and adult life. Part of the great charm of *Daphnis and Chloe* lies in this residue. "But it was only later . . . " is our world, the world of the adult, the married, settled, socialized world with its formalized altars and religions. How pleasant to recall that all this had its start in the beauty of young love.

Daphnis and Chloe, then, is clearly within our genre C. All the levels of narration operate bisociatively, procontextually, and residually. *Daphnis and Chloe* is one of the first examples of so-called *romance.* We should note that many stock romantic devices already find their place in Longus' work. There are stories within the story that act metaphorically with the whole. There are alternating scenes concentrating first on Daphnis and then on

Chloe. There is the concern with noble characters. There is the fatedness of love. And also there is the very special image of the trapped bird. Because of its phenomenology (I mean to make no assertion about literary history here), this image occurs repeatedly in romance. The trapped bird serves Tom Jones importantly in his wooing of Sophia, a wooing which is the romantic thread running through Fielding's masterpiece. In *Daphnis and Chloe,* the birds are those that perennially return to Dryas' arbor. Daphnis, searching for an excuse to see Chloe, has an imaginary dialog with her guardian:

> Then [after trapping the birds in Dryas' arbor] he made up his mind to invent some excuse and push boldly through the door; and he began to ask himself what would be the most plausible thing to say.
> "I've come to get a light for a fire."
> "Why, hadn't you got neighbours only a hundred yards away?"
> "I've come to ask for some bread."
> "But your knapsack's full of food already."
> "I want some wine."
> "Yet only a day or two ago you were busy with the vintage."
> "A wolf's been chasing me."
> "Oh? And where are the wolf's footprints?"
> "I've come to catch the birds."
> "Well, now you've caught them, so why don't you go away?"
> "I want to see Chloe."
> "Who admits a thing like that to a girl's father and mother?" (pp. 72-73).

At the very surface this dialog operates anti-contextually, for each of Daphnis' potential excuses is undercut by Dryas' response. But, we must (and do, in reading) remember that these responses are *imag-*

ined responses, imagined by the same Daphnis who proposes the excuses. Thus, the entire dialog, all a part of Daphnis' mind, serves procontextually to support the notion of the irresistibility of love which has been fated from the start of the narrative. When we say of the style of a work that its suspense is procontextual, we necessarily must mean *predominantly* procontextual, for in extended narratives all sorts of things can occur. What is important here is that the anticontextuality of the dialog (considered alone) is turned about by our knowledge of its true source, thus subordinating it to the procontextual principle of narration.[24] Indeed, were we not to do this ourselves, it might not matter, for Longus has Love do it for us. Daphnis does not actually have to use any excuse because a series of unlikely events, arranged "as if Love had taken pity on him" (p. 73), causes Dryas to come out of the house, spy Daphnis, and invite him in, into the presence of the family, and of Chloe.

When the young lovers are finally alone together, they hold a real conversation which picks up the metaphor of the bird. This conversation, unlike the imagined one, is procontextual even on the surface. The language is highly metaphorical, and the image of *melting* arranges the phenomenology in such a way that there is a strong residue.

> "It was because of you that I came, Chloe."
> "I know, Daphnis."
> "It's because of you that I'm killing those poor blackbirds."
> "Well, what do you want me to do about it?"
> "I want you to remember me."
> "By the Nymphs that I once swore by in that cave, I *do* remember you! And we'll go there the moment the snow melts."

"But there's so *much* snow, Chloe, and I'm afraid
I'll melt away before it does."
"Cheer up, Daphnis. The sun's hot enough."
"Oh, Chloe, if only it were as hot as the fire
that's burning in my heart!" (pp. 75-76).

Ultimately, one learns, the sun is as hot as the fire
burning in Daphnis' heart, for it is in the cave of the
Nymphs that the lovers finally make their marriage
bed.

The notion of romance (which we have arrived at
here structurally) is often associated with a happy ending. That the ending, like the rest of the work, leaves
a residue does not imply anything about whether the
audience will smile or weep at that ending. In
medieval romance, for example, the lovers are often
"star-crossed." This is the case in Gottfried's
Tristan.[25]

The first chapter concerns Rivalin and
Blancheflor. Rivalin is the lord of Parmenie. The
narrator, in a tone adopted from the historians,
assures us of all the ways in which Rivalin is heroic,
noble, just, and generally the epitome of the actively
administrating and fighting feudal lord. Rivalin's
whole energies are turned to the care of his fief and his
honor. And then comes Love.

Rivalin proved by his own example that a lover's
fancy acts like a free bird which, in the freedom it
enjoys, perches on the lime-twig; and when it
perceives the lime and lifts itself for flight stays
clinging by the feet. And so it spreads its wings and
makes to get away, but, as it does so, cannot brush
against the twig at any part, however lightly,
without the twig's fettering it and making it a
prisoner. So now it strikes with all its might, here,
there, and everywhere, till at last fighting itself, it
overcomes itself and lies limed along the twig. This

121

**is just how untamed fancy behaves. When it falls
into sad love-longing and love works its miracle of
love-lorn sadness on him, a lover strives to regain
his freedom: but love's clinging sweetness draws
him down and he ensnares himself in it so deeply
that, try as he may, he cannot get free of it.
So it went with Rivalin . . . (p. 52).**

Gottfried has taken the image of the trapped bird
(which plays a minor role in Longus) and turned it
into a metaphor for the theme of the entire work, love.
This controlling metaphor operates residually, for its
nexal structure can never be complete until the bird is
either dead or captured. Thus, the phenomenology of
the metaphor is structurally analogous to the action of
the entire book. In this passage already we see
suspense at all levels of narration working
procontextually: theme, plot, and character combined
in action ("Rivalin proved by his own example"), and
style. Rivalin's solution to his love-sickness is to get
captured. Although this reduces the energy with
which he can attend to affairs of state, he marries
Blancheflor (white-flower; virgin) in perfect accord
with the dictates of his society and the people of
Parmenie rejoice at the possibility of having an heir.

Still in the first chapter, Gottfried goes on to tell
us of Rivalin and Blancheflor's mutual devotion. They
are happy and beloved; all they lack is an heir.
However, before conception can occur, Rivalin's
friend, King Mark of Cornwall, asks help in fighting
off an enemy. Rivalin goes, helps turn back the
enemy, but receives a wound which promises to be
fatal. He is on a death-bed. No one is allowed to see
the dying friend of Cornwall. But Blancheflor slips
across the channel, bribes the nurse, and, disguised as
a peasant woman delivering food, comes to see her
husband.

Rivalin with great difficulty inclined his head in thanks as much as a dying man might. But Blancheflor scarcely noticed it and paid no attention, but merely sat there unseeing, and laid her cheek on Rivalin's, till for joy but also for sorrow her strength deserted her body. Her rosy lips grew wan, the hue of her flesh quite lost the glow that dwelt in it before. In her clear eyes the day turned dark and sombre as night. Thus she lay senseless in a swoon for a long time, her cheek on his cheek, as though she were dead. And when she had rallied a little from this extremity she took her darling in her arms and laying her mouth to his kissed him a hundred thousand times in a short space till her lips fired his sense and roused his mettle for love, since love resided in them. Her kisses made him gay, they brought him such vigour that he strained the splendid woman to his half-dead body, very tenderly and close. Nor was it long before they had their way and the sweet woman received a child from him. As to Rivalin he was all but dead, both of the woman and love. But for God's helping him from this dire pass he could never have lived; yet live he did, for so it was to be (pp. 57-58).

Rivalin lives on nine months in the first chapter, lives long enough to die a glorious battlefield death in the service of King Mark. Blancheflor mourns silently at his side for four days, and then delivers up her soul and a child: the infant Tristan.

This first chapter is a structural model for the entire story, and, like it, is structurally analogous to the central metaphor of the limed bird. The more extended narrative, of course, is not about Rivalin, but about his son. The liming of his son is expressed metaphorically by the famous love-potion. Tristan, like his father, serves King Mark. The youth's mission is to bring Mark the beautiful Ysolt to wife. But in transporting her to Cornwall, by accident, by fate, they share a love-potion. Tristan's liming is different from his father's, for his cannot result in capture, marriage. That would undercut all the standards of his feudal society: Tristan is Mark's sworn vassal. The only alternative for the limed bird is death. The narrative proceeds to the death not only of Tristan, but by analogy to the first chapter, of Ysolt. Tristan, mortally wounded, is lying on a tor overlooking the harbor through which Ysolt's ship must pass if she answers his call to see him once more before he dies. Ysolt has been instructed by Tristan's emissary to hoist a white sail if the wind is good, a black if there is calm. We wait to see which color will show. Tristan cannot raise himself to look, and instructs his wife (he has by this time married, despite his passion, and his wife's name too is Ysolt) to tell him the color of the sail. "The sail is all black!" (p. 352) she lies, and Tristan calls three times, "Dearest Ysolt." On the fourth call as on the fourth day of Blancheflor's mourning, Tristan dies. But, unlike the first chapter, paralleling the difference between capture and death, Tristan dies without issue. Ysolt the lover steps ashore, comes to him moments after his death, and

> She takes him in her arms and then, lying at full length, she kisses his face and lips and clasps him tightly to her. Then straining body to body, mouth to mouth, she at once renders up her spirit and of sorrow for her lover dies thus at his side.
>
> Tristan died of his longing, Ysolt because she could not come in time. Tristan died for his love; fair Ysolt because of tender pity (p. 353).

Even the words themselves (*straining, body to body, sorrow*) are the words of the first chapter. But this time there is no conception; this is an act uncompleted. And the residue carries on right out of

Gottfried (and Thomas and Wolfram) into ballad, opera, drama, folk tale, and the whole of western culture.

The residual nature of romance (even though we have defined it structurally) was obviously quite clear to Gottfried, for he did not hesitate to be sententious. (E.g., at the end of the love-potion chapter, the narrator says, in italics, that *"Love seems fairer than before and so Love's rule endures. Were Love to seem the same as before, Love's rule would soon wither away."*) The potential for such sententiousness is undoubtedly one of the reasons that so many didactic works (e.g., Sidney's *Arcadia*) are romantic in structure. There is a moralizing here that is reminiscent of, though more potent than, the moralizing tendency of works of genre A. The structural relation between genre A and genre C is clear. The reason for taking so much care in describing genre C is its numerical frequency. Apparently many people like a story that tells them something.

The most common distinguishing characteristic of romances, growing out of the structural parameters which limit the genre, is the central metaphor. In *Tristan* it is the limed bird; in *Arcadia,* the setting; in *Frankenstein,* the monster. Quite often the metaphor itself figures in the title. The residue is meant to be carried away from the book in the same way that the residue carries forward within it. We do not wait to see *what* the ending will be; our perception of the structure in the central metaphor tells us that. We wait to see *how* it comes out as we know (often, as in *Tristan,* sadly) it must.

This romantic structure is equally apparent in science fiction works like A. E. Van Vogt's *Slan* or Isaac Asimov's *Foundation* trilogy. But perhaps the best modern illustration of the close relation between

125

the romance and the popular forms of the epic and folk tale is the Western, where we always know the good guys from the bad guys. We should expect some other type of work, then, related to the picaresque and the satire (genre B) in the same way that genre C is related to genre A.

The Realistic Novel

Hawthorne thought of himself as a "romancer."

> **In the old countries, with which fiction has long been conversant, a certain conventional privilege seems to be awarded to the romancer; his work is not put exactly side by side with nature; and he is allowed a license with regard to every-day probability . . .[26]**

This license is necessary because, as we have seen in romances, things work out as we expect them to. In life, "nature," they clearly do not. Life is chaotic; nature formless. It is the mind of man, as the gestalt psychologists[27] and the modern anthropologists[28] teach us, that imposes organization on nature. Consider the following figure:

Fig. 2. Gestalt Pattern 1

Most of us will see figure 2 as a square. Once we do, it can be nothing else. There is but one context established for it. It is logically possible to conceive of the figure as four separate lines which happen to intersect, and which happen to form right angles at their intersections, but we do not. We make a context in our minds, organizing the parts into a whole.

Now consider the following figure. "Fixate," as the psychologists say, on its center.

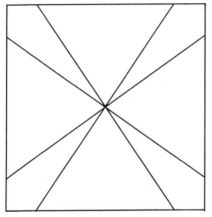

Fig. 3. Gestalt Pattern 2

At first, the organization of the figure will be quite clear. But after continued attention, a second organizational possibility will occur to one. The two possibilities are the following: the thin blades form a *propeller* which is framed by the square; the thin blades are the background, and the fat blades form a *Maltese cross* which is framed by the square. Once we have discovered the two possibilities, it is only by an effort of will that we can fix a single possibility in mind. As one stares, the two possible configurations alternate, the speed of alternation increasing as the time of staring lengthens. This is anticontextual bisociation with a residue. The two contexts enter our temporal experience of the figure, one undercutting the other, and leaving the residual feeling of ambiguity. Notice that even in looking at this "static" drawing, ambiguity occurs as the result of a temporal process. Our perception of the drawing extends through time. The identification of ambiguity as a phenomenon both directly related to bisociation and extended in time was apparent even in Koestler's original study.[29] ". . . bisociation is not the same thing as ambiguity; ambiguity is merely a subcategory of it." Koestler counters the statement of Empsonian analysis by extending the implicit assumption behind it.

> **Ambiguity is double meaning, but there is no double meaning, for example, in the word "medal" [in the story which Koestler relates]. "Medal" occurs there not in two different meanings but in two different associative** *contexts.*

The presence of many applicable associative contexts is what makes us uncertain about things in life, reminds us of the contingency of the real world, enforces the notion of chaos. This persistent problem of organization appears in man's continuing interest in eschatology (as Frank Kermode treats it)[30] on one hand, and on the "reading" of a work of art (as E. H. Gombrich treats it) on another. T. E. Hulme[31] manages to divide all philosophies into two camps: those which view the human mediation between the absolute laws of nature and the anagogical universe as absolute, and those which view that human mediation as contingent. Since the Renaissance at least, all widespread philosophies have been of the second type, which actually points to the problem of context. Is abortion murder? That depends upon context: shall we consider the fetus as a growth in the mother or as a separate and independent human being? Is *mercy killing* perhaps a contradiction in terms? Even the smallest everyday decisions come against the ambiguity of multiple contexts. Shall one have a very good piece of cake for dessert, or a mediocre cup of chocolate pudding? For a gourmet, these function within a single context, and the problem is resolved in favor of the cake. But for a child who, all things being equal, prefers pudding, the choice is difficult. And the child experiences suspense, for the ambiguity, as in figure 3, is extended in time. Unless we are functioning automatically, that is, within a single context, all things are never equal.

The inequality of contexts, the ambiguity, arises, as in figure 3, as a result of our attention. The Russian formalists[32] attached great importance to the notion of "defamiliarization." Normally we go through life treating things automatically. We do not consider the gas pedal when we drive, the manual skills involved when we eat, the street address when we return home at night. ". . . art exists that one may recover the sensation of life; it exists to make one feel things, to make the stone *stony*."[33] One of the methods of defamiliarization, and that which most closely mirrors the modern understanding of the contingency of life, is to show how something may operate in two antithetical contexts. Context carries the fictional reality. When our attention is directed so as to be made aware of the antitheses of contexts, the total fictional reality incorporates our aliterary underlying notion of reality. At least, this would be the case if we accept the conclusions of the philosophers, the critics, and the social scientists. For this reason, I would call figure 3 (which incorporates the principles of our genre D) *realistic*. There are narratives which incorporate these same principles.

We have defined *realistic,* then, as a structural property that depends upon a certain suspense structure. A realistic narrative, theoretically, would be one which exhibited anticontextual, residual bisociation at all levels of narration. But the term *realistic* already has a traditional literary use (despite its extension by Auerbach) in the genre classification of *realistic novel.* Let us examine the structural principles that lie behind the reading of works which are commonly called realistic.

The following dialogue is a bit of characterization from *A Modern Instance.*[34] Kinney is the cook at a logging camp which the newspaperman/protagonist Bartley Hubbard is visiting for a story.

"... I should call beans a brain food."

"I guess you call anything a brain food that you happen to like, don't you, Kinney?"

"No, sir," said Kinney, soberly; "but I like to see the philosophy of a thing when I get a chance. Now, there's tea, for example," he said, pointing to the great tin pot on the stove.

"Coffee, you mean," said Bartley.

"No, sir, I mean tea. That's tea; and I give it to 'em three times a day, good and strong—molasses in it, and no milk. That's a brain food, if ever there was one. Sets 'em up, right on end, every time. Clears their heads and keeps the cold out."

"I should think you were running a seminary for young ladies, instead of a logging camp," said Bartley.

"No, but look at it; I'm in earnest about tea. You look at the tea drinkers and the coffee drinkers all the world over! Look at 'em in our own country! All the Northern people and all the go-ahead people drink tea. The Pennsylvanians and the Southerners drink coffee. Why, our New England folks don't even know how to *make* coffee so it's fit to drink! And it's just so all over Europe. The Rusians drink tea, and they'd e't up those coffee-drinkin' Turks long ago, if the tea-drinkin' English hadn't kept 'em from it. Go anywheres you like in the North, and you find 'em drinkin' tea. The Swedes and Norwegians in Aroostook County drink it; and they drink it at home."

"Well, what do you think of the French and Germans? They drink coffee, and they're pretty smart, active people, too."

"French and Germans drink coffee?"

"Yes."

Kinney stopped short in his heated career of generalization, and scratched his shaggy head. "Well," he said, finally, "I guess they're a kind of a missing link, as old Darwin says" (pp. 102-3).

The initial anticontextuality is set up by the ironic bisociation of the idea of "brain food" (an old wives' tale) and "philosophy." Grossly, the diachronic structure of this segment is defined by two antithetical forms: the interview (which Bartley is trying to elicit by his ironies) and the discourse (which Kinney is trying to complete by his passion). In detail, these two sets of contexts make continual anticontextual bisociation. Bartley's first response deflates the apparent intellectuality behind Kinney's statement. Kinney's rejoinder in terms of "philosophy" operates not only against Bartley, but against the usual context for his own idea of "brain food." He points to his tea. "Coffee, you mean," is Bartley's response, a response which tells us that the liquid is so dark and strong as to be unrecognizable as tea. But Kinney asserts that it is tea, and then goes on to describe it in such a way that it might very well pass for coffee. This description makes Kinney's later line ("Why, our New England folks don't even know how to *make* coffee so it's fit to drink!") highly ironic,

131

for we do not trust his ability to judge the "fitness" of coffee, since he obviously has absurd notions about tea. Bartley's lines, too, not only in terms of the thematic context but in terms of style, are anti-contextual: "I should think you were running a seminary for young ladies, instead of a logging camp." The anticontextual bisociations could, theoretically, discharge the contexts and result in jokes, but they do not. Kinney's last rejoinder ("I guess they're a kind of a missing link, as old Darwin says.") places the old wives' tale ironically back into the context of philosophy (a word he, in light of *Darwin,* is obviously misusing ironically) and creates a residue, for it ends with the open question of classifying that *missing link.* Clearly Kinney, the philosopher, will now have much to ponder. Thus, both in style and theme, the segment uses the suspense of its diachronic structure anticontextually, bisociatively, and residually.

As a bit of character development, it follows these same parameters. We first see an assured Kinney, then a Kinney beaten down by the facts, and then a Kinney struggling against the facts to regroup his mental defenses. This bisociative anticontextuality creates a residue, and Kinney becomes a *realistic* character, the kind we could imagine transporting into other situations. His initial introduction, just six pages earlier, already sets up the way in which Kinney lives, poised between the irrefutability of fact and the appeal of philosophy. In all contexts, he struggles against fact, even at the expense of learning, in order (thus anticontextually) to preserve philosophy.

> **Kinney was the cook. He had been over pretty nearly the whole of the uninhabitable globe, starting as a gaunt and awkward boy from the Maine woods, and keeping until he came back to them in late middle life the same gross and ridiculous optimism. He**

had been at sea, and ship-wrecked on several islands in the Pacific; he had passed a rainy season at Panama, and a yellow fever season at Vera Cruz, and had been carried far into the interior of Peru by a tidal wave during an earthquake season; he was in the Border Ruffian War of Kansas, and he clung to California till prosperity deserted her after the completion of the Pacific road. Wherever he went he carried or found adversity; but, with a heart fed on the metaphysics of Horace Greeley, and buoyed up by a few wildly interpreted maxims of Emerson, he had always believed in other men, and their fitness for the terrestrial millennium, which was never more than ten days or ten miles off (pp. 96-97).

This antithesis between ideas and facts is a structural miniature of the whole novel. *A Modern Instance* plays upon a number of literary conventions in order to establish as one context an ideal world. The heroine, Marcia Gaylord, is beautiful and virginal and love-struck with Bartley. To that extent, she is reminiscent of Blancheflor. However, these characters marry, not as Rivalin and Blancheflor, but because it seems the right thing to do after they fool themselves into believing they are in love. "Afterward it was a mortification to [the townspeople] that they should not have thought at once of Bartley Hubbard and Marcia Gaylord" (p. 7). *Afterward*, after their marriage, creates a new context for the townspeople. But we have seen the unfiery romance, and realize the antithesis between the ideal of marriage and the facts of this union. The marriage proceeds in one context according to a romantic ideal. Marcia sticks with Bartley through thick and thin; they go to New York so that, through romantic struggle, Bartley can make his success as a journalist; she defends their marriage and their poverty against her squire father. But at the same time, and operating against this context, the novel bisociates a second context. Bartley is unfaithful to his wife; his success is both temporary and based on the ruthless use of people; and, even when he is making money, he refuses to care for Marcia properly, turning instead to vice. The conflict between Bartley's view of the marriage and Marcia's view stands anticontextually, and illuminates the difference between realism and romance; for Daphnis and Chloe, though they have their problems, always agree on the nature of their love.

The plot uses these characters and themes in order to progress also anticontextually, bisociatively, and residually. Marcia's fidelity is matched by Bartley's infidelity. Bartley's progressive loss of success is matched by Marcia's learning steadfast frugality. Bartley's desertion is matched by Marcia's turning herself into a Penelope. But Bartley is no Odysseus. The Squire finally tracks Bartley down and ends his daughter's legal involvement with Hubbard not through death (as is common in romance), but through divorce on the grounds of desertion. Despite the divorce, and with Bartley off the scene, Marcia will not remarry. The reader has hopes, however, for all through her suffering she has had a silent suitor, Ben Halleck. When news arrives that Bartley is finally dead, Ben writes to Atherton, the lawyer friend of the Squire's who had prosecuted the divorce, to speak of marrying the divorcee/widow. The anticontextual bisociation of style and theme is obvious in the last page as Atherton discusses the letter with his wife:

> ". . . it's terrible to think of that poor creature [Marcia] living there [in Bartley's house] by herself, with no one to look after her and her little girl; and if Ben—"
> "What do you mean, Clara? Don't you see that

his being in love with her when she was another man's wife is what he feels it to be—an indelible stain?"

"She never knew it; and no one ever knew it but you. You said it was our deeds that judged us. Didn't Ben go away when he realized his feeling for her?"

"He came back."

"But he did everything he could to find that poor wretch [Bartley], and he tried to prevent the divorce. Ben is morbid about it; but there is no use in our being so."

"There was a time when he would have been glad to profit by a divorce."

"But he never did. You said the will didn't count. And now she is a widow, and any man may ask her to marry him."

"Any man but the one who loved her during her husband's life. That is, if he is such a man as Halleck. Of course it isn't a question of gross black and white, mere right and wrong; there are degrees, there are shades. There might be redemption for another sort of man in such a marriage; but for Halleck there could only be loss— deterioration—lapse from the ideal. I should think that he might suffer something of this even in her eyes—"

"Oh, how hard you are! I wish Ben hadn't asked your advice. Why, you are worse than he is! You're *not* going to write that to him?"

Atherton flung the letter upon the table, and drew a troubled sigh. "Ah, I don't know! I don't know!"

And so the last line leaves us (residually) with a final conflict of contexts.

This line, "I don't know!" is reminiscent of the syncrisis of time and place in the famous last line of another novel which is traditionally called realistic,

The Ambassadors:[35] " 'Then there we are!' said Strether" (emphasis mine). The residuality of realistic novels, which are anticontextual, parallels the residuality of the romance. Whereas in the latter we are tempted to think, "And so they lived on together," in the former we think, "And so it is in our lives." We think this, even when the facts of the characters' lives have nothing in common with our own, because the structure of their lives (the emergence and development of which creates the suspense of the novel) is the same as the structure of our lives, the structure of ambiguity, irony. The perception of their story is structurally equivalent to the perception of the cross and the propeller in figure 3.

This point becomes clear when we examine any novel which tradition calls realistic. A prime example of this is *Germinal*.[36] Readers of Zola's novel are continually struck by the way in which he takes images, which phenomenologically operate one way, and puts them to contrary uses. At the simplest level, the book serves as an indictment of the social system which dehumanizes men in the service of the mines of France. Our sympathies clearly lie with the miners. However, the miners live a black and subterranean life, while the owners live above ground in the air and light. As Bachelard's studies have pointed out, up and down, white and black, form automatic metaphors for good and evil. These were the images that Hawthorne the romancer used in his dichotomies which bound together "The Great Carbuncle." Zola is no romancer. He creates his sense of realism using these images in alien contexts, thus creating an anticontextual bisociation, the "degrees" and "shades" that Atherton mentions. The daughter of the owners, Cecile, is always in the light and wearing a white dress, much like Phoebe (light) in *The House of Seven Gables*. However, she is not goodness. She sees, but does not understand, the plight of the miners. Out traveling one day in the family coach, she is moved to help one, and so (like a bourgeois Marie Antoinette), she offers the cake which she has with her, an ineffectual type of aid. But her motivation is real, and so there is a residue in her characterization. One continues to be troubled by her acceptance of her father's admonition that the cake would spoil the pauper. In the same way, following the ironic reversal of convention that creates the anticontextuality of the work, there is Catherine, the romantic heroine, the girl whom we should sympathize with. Her physical presence, however (she is described as quite boylike) undercuts this, and her promiscuity goes a long way to destroy it. And yet, her promiscuity serves a real need for the miners, and to that extent this coal-covered boy/girl is still a better heroine than Cecile.

The plot, as well as the style and theme, works anticontextually. The central event of the book is the miners' strike for better pay and conditions. After much hardship, the strike is broken, the miners lose all and return to an even more impoverished and degrading existence. This failure motivates the protagonist, Etienne, to quit, ironically achieving success by abandoning the problem. The last scene of the novel shows him miles from town. He still feels the miners beneath his feet, burrowing horizontally to extend the honey-comb mine beneath the countryside of France. In this context of despair, the book ends with

On this youthful morning, in the fiery rays of the sun, the whole country was alive with this sound [mining]. Men were springing up, a black avenging host was slowly germinating in the furrows, thrusting upwards for the harvests of future ages.

And very soon their germination would crack the earth asunder (p. 499).

This, of course, we have no reason to accept as fact, although we wish it in theory, for the "crack" in the book closes down again to bury the miners in even more misery. Zola associates this anticontextuality with the notion of germination, a seed coming forth from below. Thus, the anticontextual bisociations leave a powerful residue, Etienne walking off into the sun*rise* (yet defeated) and the cycle of life that germination represents coming to stand for the continuing antithesis between the way men should live and the way they do live.

All of these structures containing anticontextual bisociation with residue can be found in a single paragraph. In the one below, this particular use of suspense dominates all levels of narration at once: plot, character, style, and theme. Souvarine is a Communist. Maheude and Zacharie represent two generations of miners. In order to attack the owners, Souvarine has just blown up the mine, although it is filled with the people he says he intends his revolution to aid. He watches the ground collapse into a "crater" and fill with water, undoubtedly drowning many of the workers.

At that moment Souvarine rose to his feet on the shaken slag-heap. He had recognized Maheude and Zacharie [who had not entered the mine yet] sobbing together in the presence of this total collapse which must be pressing with its stupendous weight on the heads of those poor wretches dying down below. He threw away his last cigarette and walked off into the darkness without so much as a glance behind. His shadowy form dwindled and merged into the night. He was bound for the unknown, over yonder, calmly going to deal violent

destruction wherever dynamite could be found to blow up cities and men. Doubtless, on that day when the last expiring bourgeois hear the very stones of the streets exploding under their feet, he will be there (p. 453).

Here again, we have anticontextual bisociation with a residue. The novel, which tradition has called *realistic,* exhibits a diachronic structure analogous to that which the theory asserts would be perceived as realistic. Using the theory, then, we can establish hypotheses about this genre. We would predict (and it is of course true) that the anticontextuality expresses itself in irony and ambiguity. We would also predict that novels that do not have the factitious content of *A Modern Instance* or *Germinal,* still would leave us with a sense of realism if the structural arrangement of their content followed the parameters of genre D. This, of course, is the case in something like John Hawkes' *Second Skin.* By elucidating the dependence of novels traditionally called realistic upon a particular theoretical structure, we are then able to do two important things. First, we can put the question of verisimilitude of action and description into its proper subordinate place. It is merely a function of the structural arrangement and treatment of the details, and not of their inherent believability. And second, we can point to the kind of suspense that keeps us going through a realistic novel. It is the attraction that makes us study something even as simple as figure 3.

The Comedy and the Melodrama

It is not possible to find works that *completely* fulfill the parameters of either genre E or genre F. Both of these genres are defined by *discharge,* that is, suspense operates in the structure to lead us to a bisociation that has no diachronic residue. Such is the

139

case in the joke. But even in the joke, the complete discharge can occur only once; that is the structural significance of the punch line. The style (for example) of the narration leading up to that punch line cannot truly discharge the contexts (although its latent content allows for the final discharge) for the first discharge would complete the structure and end the narrative. In extended narrative forms, like the novel, the impossibility of continuous discharge occurring simultaneously at all levels of narration prevents us from finding works that fulfill our structural parameters.

Instead of looking for such works then, we should look for works in which discharge is a principle, but expect to find it now in plot, then in style, now in character, then in theme. Such a work would strike the reader subliminally as a continuous *series* of minor discharges, while no single bisociation, with the exception of the last one of the work, could operate on all levels at once. However, although we should not expect to find, in any passage, discharge at all levels of narration, we should expect to be able to locate latent structures within that passage which allow for later discharges at all levels of narration.

The necessary continuity of at least one level of narration at any given time allows us to talk about the *voice* of the narration, or, anthropomorphizing, the *narrator,* a notion that Wayne Booth[37] justifiably calls the "implied author." It is tautological to assert that all narratives have narrators. The continuing and felt subliminal presence of the narrator is of paramount importance. It is his use of "I" in *The Narrative of A. Gordon Pym* (see pp. 60 ff.) that leads to the failure of the last pages of Poe's book. The continuing presence of the voice always mitigates the sense of discharge we feel at any given point within an extended narrative.

If there were some continuing presence other than voice to hold us to the work of art, then it might be possible for a work to fulfill the structural parameters of genres E and F completely. In drama, the radical of presentation[38] is quite different from that of narrative. Whereas in the latter we are aware of *voice* as presence, in drama we are aware of *physical* presence. The joke is a necessarily short form, but burlesque (a structural equivalent in drama) can be quite extended. In a sense, the continued physical presence of the actors leaves a residue to carry the performance forward, while in narration, which has only language, when all the language explodes, the presence of the voice disappears.

For this reason, in discussing narratives of our discharging genres, it is useful to borrow terms from drama. Such a nomenclature should remind us of three things: these narratives cannot fulfill all their structural principles simultaneously; these structures are not as numerically common in narrative as are the structures of our first four genres; the members of these last two genres will quite commonly show a structure that assimilates other structures in order to maintain the voice and thus continue the narrative. With these reservations, we can investigate the nature of the books that might inhabit the never-never land of our discharging genres.

Since the paradigm cases for genre E must necessarily be nonexistent, the best we can hope to do is indicate their nature. This procedure, therefore, cannot exhaustively describe any real narrative, but it can help us define a narrative ideal whose existence is important in describing real works. Such a theoretical notion is analytically useful in criticism in the same way that the ideal notion of *asymptote* is useful in geometry. A hyperbola never, in a finite distance, reaches its asymptote, but we cannot describe any hyperbola without resorting to the ideal of asymptotic approach. There are works clearly related to romance, genre C, which share the properties of bisociation and procontextuality, but seems structurally different from romance. The problem of mixing of genres in general will be taken up in chapter 4. Here we are concerned with works that change romance by having their metaphoric bisociations, *as much as possible,* replace residue with discharge. *Bleak House*[39] is such a work.

As Edwin Muir[40] points out, novels like those which Dickens produced depend for their effect on the great multiplicity of characters and the extraordinary complication of the plot machinery. My *in*complete listing for *Bleak House,* for example, notes ten different and important settings and seventy-six separate characters. Summarizing such a work would be tedious. However, I hope the wide circulation of the novel will relieve me of that responsibility. Anyone who has read the work must share with me the impression that is created throughout: we are in the hands of a narrator who knows how things will turn out; everything *will* turn out; and all the loose ends will somehow be brought into the master fabric of the novel. Consider the opening paragraph:

> **London. Michaelmas Term lately over, and the Lord Chancellor sitting in Lincoln's Inn Hall. Implacable November weather. As much mud in the streets, as if the waters had but newly retired from the face of the earth, and it would not be wonderful to meet a Megalosaurus, forty feet long or so, waddling like an elephantine lizard up Holborn Hill. Smoke lowering down from**

chimneypots, making a soft black drizzle, with flakes of soot in it as big as full-grown snow-flakes—gone into mourning, one might imagine, for the death of the sun. Dogs, undistinguishable in mire. Horses, scarcely better; splashed to their very blinkers. Foot passengers, jostling one another's umbrellas, in a general infection of ill-temper, and losing their foothold at street-corners, where tens of thousands of other foot passengers have been slipping and sliding since the day broke (if this day ever broke), adding new deposits to the crust upon crust of mud, sticking at those points tenaciously to the pavement, and accumulating at compound interest (p. 1).

There is a principle of plenitude operating here that does much to reduce the possible residue of both the image- and syntax-structures. Consider how many motifs enter the paragraph: the city (*London*), the legal system (*Michaelmas Term, Lord Chancellor, Lincoln's Inn Hall*), the grime of overcrowding (*mud, flakes of soot,* and so forth), the badness of man (the allusion to Noah's flood, the foot passengers' universal *ill-temper*), the bestiality of man (*dogs, horses,* and *foot passengers* in parallel), the unmanageability of size (*Megalosaurus, crust upon crust of mud*), blindness (*death of the sun, indistinguishable, blinkers*), and the economic system (*accumulating at compound interest*). This last, when it is perceived, is anticontextual, for it follows a series of meteorological, psychological, and other naturalistic images. But by ending the series this way, the narrator creates the impression that the description has been total, and there is no significant residue left. Compare this setting with the discovery by Lamon of the infant Daphnis (see page 116). The last detail here caps the description, and all the motifs discharge into the single notion of London.

We see that this single notion alone is residual. It does carry through the book. Complete discharge at all levels would end *Bleak House* after the first paragraph. But a great deal is discharged here; the metaphoric images bisociate in such a way as to dissipate themselves, and leave us only the single motif of *London*. It is this motif which the narrator picks up as he continues:

> **Fog everywhere. Fog up the river, where it flows among green aits [small river islands] and meadows; fog down the river, where it rolls defiled among the tiers of shipping, and the waterside pollutions of a great and dirty city (p. 1).**

Structurally, this second paragraph is continuing in the manner of the first. Picking up on the one residual motif, it can move paratactically into *fog*. The two other motifs here of economic system (*shipping*) and grime (*dirty city*) need to be articulated again, and they need to be attached to the single undischarged, residual, motif of *London*. Thus, the style largely fulfills the parameters of genre E, though no description of the work is sufficient which does not point to the irony used to maintain the voice.

In the same way, the character development is bisociative, procontextual, and discharging. Each character is delineated metaphorically. For example, we "have" Mr. Quale when we take the hint from his name (hunted bird, and Klang association with *quake* and *frail*) and see his abject admiration for the ("telescopic") philanthropy of Mrs. Jellyby. The "hint of characterization"[41] in almost all character names of Dickens's novels is a continuing narrative device. These metaphorically defined characters continue through the novel doing just what would be appropriate to them. Good guys are good guys and villains are villains. This much Dickens has in common with the procontextuality of romance. But the bisociations here largely discharge their contexts; the Dickensian tag needs to be restated to revivify the character. The interrelations of the characters pile up in obvious preparation for a final discharge. Charley, for example, becomes the maid of Esther Summerson. But Charley is Neckett's daughter; Neckett, because he is employed by Coavinses, the sheriff, has to dun Harold Skimpole for money; Skimpole is the freeloading guest/protege of John Jarndyce; Jarndyce has two young wards, Richard and Ada; in order to care for them, he hires a governess, Esther Summerson; thus, the connection that allows for Charley's employment. However, Charley also knows Caddy Jellyby, who happens to be a friend of Esther; thus, a second connection. Such an account of barely ten percent of the characters of the book will serve to remind a reader of Dickens of the sense of "web" that develops, that everything is on a collision course. As we pointed out, we cannot expect discharge all the time; but the continuing reminder of a latent structure that will only achieve resolution through discharge should cue us that the procontextual bisociations here are different from those we find in romance.

At this point, we have moved from character into plot. It is in plot that the discharging nature of the procontextual bisociations of Dickens becomes clearest. In almost all his novels, the last chapter manages to account for and dispose of every character who is left alive. Although it is too long to quote, any cursory reading of the last pages of *Bleak House* will confirm this. It is the "disposing of" characters that makes the level of character in works of genre E so different from that in works of genre C. At the end of *Daphnis and Chloe* we find the image-structures building up an idea of firstness; at the end of *Tristan,* we have an incomplete act which we know will remain incomplete forever. At the end of *Bleak House,* however, we have everyone settled in; society has been reconstituted. This is not the first, but the last; and nothing is incomplete.

I would like to advance two critical truisms: *comedy* is concerned with the re-establishment of society; Dickens is a comic novelist. Because these truisms are so ingrained in critics, and because *comedy* is really a term from drama, a concept which cannot be *completely* realized in narrative, I would call the ideal theoretical structure of works of genre E *comedy.* In this usage, we should say that the previous analysis of *Bleak House* points out that on the level of character and plot the work is a comedy, though the style, through use of some irony, deviates from the structural definition of comedy in order to maintain the narrative voice. Such a structural definition, of course, does not dictate any necessary concern for happy endings or humor. However, since the bisociations are procontextual, the subliminal context has foisted on us the acceptance of just that society which will reach a stasis in the final bisociation. Thus, the final discharge should please us, although we certainly need not laugh. On the other hand, since the bisociations are the kind we can accept happily, they often may strike us as humorous. This is obviously the case in Dickens.

The theme of *Bleak House* is chancery. This theme is obviously treated comically. Chancery affects lives in all contexts (bisociation), is consistent in its sluggish operation (procontextuality), and finally, through the intervention of Jarndyce, becomes inconsequential (discharge). Thus, theme, like plot, character, and (almost) style, is structurally comic and works according to the same type of suspense that all comic structures create: the anticipation of the "ah yes! *that's* how it fits!" This same anticipation is similarly rewarded at the end of Austen's novels, and she, like Dickens, is traditionally considered a writer of comedy.

The last chapter of *Emma,* like the last of *Bleak House,* disposes of all the characters. The last paragraph of the book[42] illustrates the structural principles of the whole:

> **The wedding [of Knightley and Emma] was very much like other weddings, where the parties have no taste for finery or parade; and Mrs. Elton, from the particulars detailed by her husband [who officiated], thought it all extremely shabby, and very inferior to her own.—"Very little white satin, very few lace veils; a most pitiful business!—Selina would stare when she heard of it."—But, in spite of these deficiencies, the wishes, the hopes, the confidence, the predictions of the small band of true friends who witnesses the ceremony, were fully answered in the perfect happiness of the union.**

Although the structure of this paragraph is clearly comic, we would want to say that Austen is a different *kind* of comic novelist than Dickens. In Austen the irony is quite heavy. ". . . very much like other weddings," shows a detachment on the part of the narrator that is anticontextual, for it is the narrator's arrangements of motifs that have made Emma our heroine.[43] Mrs. Elton's remarks are clearly anti-contextual. However, "in spite of these deficiencies," the narrator validates the marriage and, unlike the narrator of *Tristan,* completes the final action, thus giving us a comic discharge.

Yet, besides the reliance on stylistic irony, there is another difference between the work of Austen and the work of Dickens. The former seems somehow more detached, cleaner; her work gives a more finished and unified impression. I would suggest that this comes from Austen's continual emphasis on the society. (Here I mean to make an intuitive and nonstructural distinction parallel to the distinctions made for genres A and B.) In this last paragraph of *Emma,* although we have the marriage of the two principle characters, by reporting it at third hand through the wife of the clergyman, the marriage takes on the air of a public act, an act that involves the whole of society. In the last pages of *Bleak House* (p. 665) our narrator, Esther, disposes of all the characters, and then surfaces to consider herself. She has just married a young physician; he speaks:

> **"And don't you know that you are prettier than you ever were?"**
> **I did not know that; I am not certain that I know it now. But I know that my dearest little pets are very pretty, and that my darling is very beautiful, and that my husband is very handsome, and that my guardian has the brightest and most benevolent face that ever was seen; and that they can very well do without much beauty in me—even supposing—**

The catalog of beauties puts everyone finally into his place and we have a last comic disposition of the characters. However, we are reminded that Esther reeks of false modesty. She is disposed of in the last line (though the broken syntax has that hint of stylistic anticontextuality that marks Dickens), but this disposition emphasizes her and her alone. This sets her apart from society. It seems to me that when usually comic structures, as in this line, emphasize the individual at the expense of the society, we call them *melodramatic*. This is what we feel when Stephen Blackpool dies,[44] when Em'ly is found,[45] when Esther marries. The term *melodrama*, like *comedy*, is drawn from the theater. It reminds us, then, that there can be no pure melodrama in narrative from a structural point of view. But by giving melodrama a structural definition, we can say that genre E contains a range of works that goes from comedy to melodrama. Thus, although Dickens and Austen are clearly within genre E, we would want to point out two things about their relationship: Dickens is more melodramatic than Austen; and Austen is more ironic than Dickens.

The Tragedy and the Joke

In chapter 2 we analyzed the *joke* at great length, and saw that structurally it is bisociative, anticontextual, and discharging. Thus, it clearly falls within our genre F. If we intend to continue to draw our nomenclature from drama, it might be better to call works that exhibit these structures *burlesques*. However, since the joke is such a common literary phenomenon, and since Koestler's initial analysis used joke, let us keep that term while remembering that the same restrictions apply to it as to our terms *comedy* and *melodrama* (see above). Further, the joke is necessarily a short form. An extended narrative that fulfilled the structure of the joke completely would be impossible. We can, however, have the joke stand as the ideal toward which some long forms tend. *Tristram Shandy* is one example.

We have already described (pp. 54 ff.) how the style of *Tristram Shandy* operates: each sentence is convoluted, disjunctive, and periodic. That is, the structural parameters are (respectively) bisociative, anticontextual, and discharging. The same is also true for character (which depends upon an absurd collection of ironic hobbyhorses) and plot (which depends upon mad incident and outrageous coincidence).[46] However, as we needed to describe Dickens by showing in which way he deviates from the theoretical structure of comedy in order to maintain voice, in *Tristram Shandy,* part of another discharging genre, we must note how the work deviates from the structure of the joke. This deviation is in the structure of thematic development.

Unlike the levels of style, character, and plot, the theme of *Tristram Shandy* only partially discharges. We may divide the theme of Lockean association into two parts: the conflict between clock time and psychological time; and the conflict between physical causality and mental connection. At any given point in the narrative, only one of these discharges. Consider, for example,

> . . .—Sir, replied Dr. *Slop,* it would astonish you to know what improvements we have made of late years in all branches of obstetrical knowledge, but particularly in that one single point of the safe and expeditious extraction of the *foetus,*—which has received such lights, that for my part (holding up his hands) I declare I wonder how the world has—I

wish, quoth my uncle *Toby,* **you had seen what prodigious armies we had in** *Flanders* **(p. 105).**

Here, the conflict between physical causality and mental connection discharges in the joke (which depends upon Uncle Toby's hobbyhorse); but the conflict between clock time and psychological time does not. "I wonder how the world has—" puts us back in time, into a past whose answers can be found reasonably among the camp followers of the "prodigious armies" at the battle of Flanders. The only joke of the work which discharges on all levels, including both phases of the theme, is the last:

L __d! said my mother, what is all this story about?—A Cock and a BULL, said *Yorick*—**And one of the best of its kind, I ever heard (p. 478).**

Thus, we can say that *Tristram Shandy* has the structure of a joke on three out of four levels, but that, except at the end, only one of the thematic threads at a time discharges. It is the persistence of at least part of the theme that allows for the maintenance of voice.

Structurally, the discharging, anticontextual bisociation functions in the same way that the recognition does in dramatic tragedy. We all recall the terror of Oedipus' discovery. Although the following distinction does not completely describe the relation of tragedy to joke, it is useful: when a work of genre F concerns only the individual, the discharge releases laughter; when it reflects on all of society, the discharge releases "fear and pity." Aristotle made sure to include in his definition of tragedy the prescription that the protagonist be of high estate. As the noble setting was important to the satire of *Howleglas,* Oedipus's royalty is important to his tragedy; that he is the king carries with it the whole force of our social

151

involvement. Tom Lehrer[47] has deflated Oedipus by emphasizing him as an individual. By treating him in a light song, Lehrer identifies Oedipus, the emblem of society, with a figure of fun. The following lyrics are intended to be sung in a spirited, honky-tonk way:

> There once was a man named Oedipus Rex.
> You might have heard about his strange complex.
> It's written down in Freud's index
> That he lo-o-oved his MOTHer!
>
> . . . .
> . . . .
> He loved his mother like no other,
> His daughter was his sister and his son was his brother.
> The thing on which you can depend is,
> *He* sure knew who a boy's best friend is!
>
> When he saw what he had done,
> He tore his eyes out, one by one:
> A tragic end to a loyal son
> Who lo-o-oved his MOTHer!

There are very great differences between a joke and a tragedy, but the differences are in attitude, emphasis, and so forth, rather than in structure. The man slipping on the banana peel is humorous, but not when we identify with that man as our cultural ideal. Consider the story that Norman Holland tells:

> The young executive had taken $100,000 from his company's safe, lost it playing the stock market, and now he was certain to be caught, and his career ruined. In despair, down to the river he went.
>
> He was just clambering over the bridge railing when a gnarled hand fell upon his arm. He turned and saw an ancient crone in a black cloak, with wrinkled face and stringy hair. "Don't jump," she rasped. "I'm a witch, and I'll grant you three

wishes for a slight consideration."

"I'm beyond help," he replied, but he told her his troubles, anyway.

"Nothing to it," she said, cackling, and she passed her hand before his eyes, "You now have a personal bank account of $200,000!" She passed her hand again. "The money is back in the company vault!" She covered his eyes for the third time. "And you have just been elected first vice-president."

The young man, stunned speechless, was finally able to ask, "What—what is the consideration I owe you?"

"You must spend the night making love to me," she smiled toothlessly.

The thought of making love to the old crone revolted him, but it was certainly worth it, he thought, and together they retired to a nearby motel. In the morning, the distasteful ordeal over, he was dressing to go home when the old crone in the bed rolled over and asked, "Say, sonny, how old are you?"

"I'm forty-two years old," he said, "Why?"

"Ain't you a little old to believe in witches?"[48]

Indeed, he is, and so are we, but we accept the notion of *witch* subliminally in order to read the narrative. The fact that witches do not exist creates a latent attitude which allows for the final humorous discharge. The small store we put in the protagonist leaves us free to laugh. However, were the held-out hope the "drunken post-boys in troikas," and were we involved with the character, as we are with Vanka, our reaction would not be laughter. By making the hero the representative of the particular society that the work forces us to accept, the discharge takes on a tremendous weight, and the bisociation is not humorous, but pathetic.

Tragedy is another concept imported from drama. As with narrative comedy, the continuing presence of the voice mitigates the effects of the discharge and we find no actual narrative that emphasizes the society and still fulfills the structural parameters of genre F *completely.* We can, however, speak of works that approach this. *Death in Venice* is such a work.

Even in the first paragraph, we can see concerns larger than Aschenbach impinging on the development of his character and marking the social emphasis of the story (an emphasis latent in the title). The irony of the style contributes toward anti-contextual bisociation.

> Gustave Aschenbach—or von Aschenbach, as he had been known officially since his fiftieth birthday—had set out alone from his house in Prince Regent Street, Munich, for an extended walk. It was a spring afternoon in that year of grace 19—, when Europe sat upon the anxious seat beneath a menace that hung over its head for months. Aschenbach had sought the open soon after tea. He was over-wrought by a morning of hard, nerve-taxing work, work which had not ceased to exact his uttermost in the way of sustained concentration, conscientiousness, and tact; and after the noon meal found himself powerless to check the onward sweep of the productive mechanism within him, that *motus animi continuus* in which, according to Cicero, eloquence resides. He had sought but not found relaxation in sleep—though the wear and tear upon his system had come to make a daily nap more and more imperative—and now undertook a walk, in the hope that air and exercise might send him back refreshed to a good evening's work.[49]

The concept of exhausting work which requires "concentration, conscientiousness, and *tact*" already begins the anticontextual development of the character. The theme of bodily inability to fulfill one's ideals is latent here, preparing for its discharge in Aschenbach's death. The style of the whole paragraph is anticontextual. Notice, for example, the clash between *grace* and *anxious* or *menace*. With this type of narrative voice, we learn by the end of the paragraph that Aschenbach's wish for refreshment is futile, and this knowledge of ours subsumes all the previously learned information. Thus, the style, the character, and the theme discharge *nearly* completely, leaving only an impression about the futility of the walk. This residue in plot is what keeps *Death in Venice* from fulfilling the ideal structure of tragedy; but this residue is the necessary carry-over to maintain the narrative voice. The residual treatment of plot runs throughout the novel, up until the end itself, while the other levels of narration proceed according to the parameters of genre F. The *officially* of the second line and the reference to Cicero already make the narrative concern a large social one, a concern which is artfully maintained throughout. This concern comes through strongly in the last two paragraphs. Tadzio is the youth whom Aschenbach loves, but cannot have. In these final paragraphs, Aschenbach makes one last attempt to touch the fleeing concept of youth:

> There he [Tadzio] stayed a little, with bent head, tracing figures in the wet sand with one toe; then stepped into the shallow water, which at its deepest did not wet his knees; waded idly through it and reached the sand-bar. Now he paused again, with his face turned seaward; and next began to move slowly leftwards along the narrow strip of sand the sea left bare. He paced there, divided by an expanse

> of water from the shore, from his mates by his moody pride; a remote and isolated figure, with floating locks, out there in sea and wind, against the misty inane. Once more he paused to look: with a sudden recollection, or by an impulse, he turned from the waist up, in an exquisite movement, one hand resting on his hip, and looked over his shoulder at the shore. The watcher [Aschenbach, who has studied all these movements before and whose watching violates the very idea of *remote and isolated*] sat just as he had sat that time in the lobby of the hotel when first the twilit grey eyes had met his own. He rested his head against the chair-back and followed the movements of the figure out there, then lifted it, as it were in answer to Tadzio's gaze. It sank on his breast, the eyes looked out beneath their lids, while his whole face took on the relaxed and brooding expression of deep slumber. It seemed to him the pale and lovely Summoner out there smiled at him and beckoned; as though, with the hand he lifted from his hip, he pointed outward as he hovered on before into an immensity of richest expectation.
>
> Some minutes passed before anyone hastened to the aid of the elderly man sitting there collapsed in his chair. They bore him to his room. And before nightfall a shocked and respectful world received the news of his decease (p. 75).

The sudden change from Aschenbach's perspective to society's makes the narrative discharge at all levels anticontextually. "The world" will *not* receive the true news of Aschenbach's death, for it is not privy to the anguish which we have seen. The plot (traveling) ends here in the completion of Aschenbach's life, while the theme of the search for youth is discharged anticontextually by the protagonist's final futile projections onto Tadzio. This action completes the character in the same way, and the clash of the

ultimate paragraph against the penultimate main-
tains the anticontextuality of style. The discharge of
decease is clearly different from the residual *"I don't
know"* of Howells's realistic novel. Were we to consider just the ending, we should say that *Death in
Venice* fulfills the structural parameters of genre F,
and that it is a tragedy.

However, it is not purely a tragedy, for as its first
paragraph shows, the plot operates residually.
Aschenbach is carried closer and closer to his failed
meeting with Tadzio by a series of men (the traveller,
the ticket seller, the gondolier, the mountebank) each
described in similar terms ("curled back his lips,"
p. 22). The sameness of the progress is neither discharging nor anticontextual. It is the regularity of plot
(which is our least concern in this novel anyway) that
allows for the maintenance of the narrative voice.

Thus, we can say that genre F contains works
which are never purely fulfilled, but whose structures
fall impurely along a range from tragedy to joke, from
social to individual. If we recognize that the ranges of
genres A, B, E, and F are not differentiated by structural principles, and if we remember that the generic
names of works in genres E and F represent ideals that
are not achievable in narrative, then we can compress
the conclusions of this study of structure into a chart,
like figure 1 (p. 91), this time giving not theoretic
generic categories, but actual ones. Since each of the
defining principles of these categories incorporates
some notion about diachronic structure, about the
functioning of subliminal suspense, this grid will serve
to distribute narratives according to the affect of their
use of suspense. Such a grid is figure 4. The (I) in
parentheses denotes the end of the range of works
within a genre that emphasizes the individual; the (S)
in parentheses denotes the end of the range of works

within a genre that emphasizes the society. The works in parentheses exemplify the type of suspense implied by the structural parameters that define the genre.

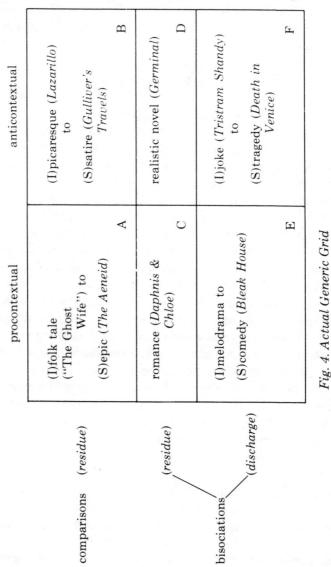

Fig. 4. Actual Generic Grid

IV

"And Then
I Wrote..."
*Possible
Directions*

This study has been based on a number of positions
which I have endeavored to make overt. First, that
subliminal suspense is integral to the experience of
any narrative which we read voluntarily; second, that
our perceptions of a narrative share much with our
perceptions of phenomena in general; third, that it is
easier to discuss and learn about anything (either
suspense or the corpus of narrative) if we can analyze
the subject of our concern by the application of exten-
sively defined generic principles. The immediate
value of such an investigation then would be the light
that the principles cast on the several objects of study,
and the light that the attendant analyses reflect on
the principles. I hope the reader has been rewarded for
his efforts thus far by some new insight into both the
phenomenon of suspense and narrative in general.

But, in this investigation in particular, because
the generic principles are grounded in a theoretical
understanding of the way a reader's mind functions,
the analysis is implicitly not just of particular
narratives, but of something that is pervasive in man.

Our specific concern has been with suspense, with the workings of diachronic structure. I have treated these subjects as rigorously as I am able. I could not bring similar knowledge to bear on the "pervasive something" that this study implies. However, because there is this something, I should like to speculate on other possible literary investigations which this study might facilitate.

The Historical Development of Genres
We can find, in any of our genres, works written at almost any time in recorded history. In romance, for example, we find both *Daphnis and Chloe* and *Tristan,* works separated, perhaps in more ways than one, by a millennium. The continuing production of romance by a practicing author today tends to indicate that once a genre (as defined structurally) appears, it persists. That is, even if we assume that within the history of a given literary community one genre develops *after* another, the development of the new genre does not obviate the effectiveness of the old genre. Still, we could look for the earliest example of each genre, and perhaps discover that there is a logic to the *emergence* of generic possibilities in narrative.

If there is such a development, I would speculate that works of genres A and B appear before works of other genres, and that the decisive factor in the emergence of those other genres is the practice of writing. It is relatively easy, as anyone who has spontaneously composed a bedtime story for a child knows, to construct an extended narrative *if* one can keep in mind the nature of the story that one wishes to tell. One would guess that in a narrative which depends upon a single context, this problem would be much more easily overcome than in a narrative which requires a multiplicity of contexts. Thus, nothing structurally like *Daphnis and Chloe* should exist in an illiterate culture. Lord's study of the Yugoslavs seems to bear this out, as do my own readings in ethnography.

But consider the *Odyssey*. This is not a pure example of genre A. All levels of narration, it is true, function according to those structural parameters, but there are really two plots, not one. The Odysseus plot and the Telemachus plot are parallel, and each is both procontextual and comparative, but there are indeed two plots. This is not the case in the epics which Lord recorded. One may guess then, as Lord concludes, that not only was the *Odyssey* an oral epic created by a poet dictating to a scribe, but that this process was accomplished in a long and leisurely fashion, that the scribe read back to the poet what they had done the day before, and that by so doing, the scribe helped the poet keep more in mind than he would have been able to in an oral performance. This multiplication of plot is a step on the way from genre A to genre C; the existence of writing begins to open new possibilities to the narrative artist. By the time we get to Longus (third century A.D.), we have a narrative artist who can himself write and who composes his works not in oral performance, but directly on paper.

After Gutenberg, however, as McLuhan has pointed out, the general consumer of narrative became less and less a listener and more and more a reader. The artists, of course, had long since become writers. But with this change in the audience, generic preferences must have changed. Today we give folk tales to children to read. The adult, trained, reading consumer prefers the structurally more complex genres. Today's best-seller list includes works of genres C and D more than any others. This does not mean that "The Ghost Wife" does not work for a modern reader, but it strikes us as somehow *thin*. All of our discussion has been based on a sympathetic, voluntary reading of narratives, and it seems, judging from book sales, that the voluntary reading of folk tales has been far outstripped by the voluntary reading of romances.

In some respects, such a prediction about the results of a study of the historical development of genres is too simple. The local details of that history surely will reflect numerous pressures. Race, moment, and milieu are not trivial concerns. However, if there is any value in this prediction, it is in the way it points to the relation between the development of narrative and the development of the human mind. Evidence for such a history would have to be drawn not only from the texts, but from other disciplines. Daphnis's imaginary conversation (p. 119), those familiar with anthropology will note, is composed of highly ritualized responses. It starts with, "I've come to get a light for a fire." Dryas's imagined response is, "Why, hadn't you got neighbors only a hundred yards away?" The first is a formulaic expression of greeting in agricultural society;[1] the second is a manifestation of territoriality.[2] Within the history of the genre of romance, we would expect that the more wholly literary productions would dispense with such formulae. This seems to be the case in the middle ages; it is certainly so by the time we get to Scott or Cooper. We should be able to observe, then, not only the gross development of the ways of thinking, but the details of what those thoughts were.

In line with this, I would like to make a further speculation about such a history. Linguists distinguish between language *competence* and language *performance*.[3] Competence has to do with what we know about the language; performance with what we do with it. Consider the following sentence: "I saw a deg in the street yesterday." Because we share a competence in English, a reader can correct such typographical performance problems in his own head, and thus read the sentence as, "I saw a *dog* in the street yesterday." Competence is part of the equipment of all native speakers of English; performance, on the other hand varies from individual to individual. If, for example, the first sentence had read, "I saw a dug in the street yesterday," then readers who did not know that *dug* is an English word would correct it to *dog* as if it were a performance problem, though in fact the correction would be their own performance problem; readers who did know the word would read on, wondering only whether the writer meant human or animal dug; and finally, for people with certain dialects, *dug* might have been accepted *un*corrected as *dog,* because of their homophony within those dialects.

As we have noted, it is experimentally true that intelligibility increases when the listener has an idea of the context of a given utterance. One may speculate that procontextual structures inherently provide a listener with a surer means to an understanding of the relevant context than do anticontextual ones. This may be why children do not learn to understand jokes until the age of six or seven (although to mimic adults, they laugh nonetheless).[4] Anticontextuality presents greater performance problems than procontextuality. We have all heard someone tell a joke at a party, and then watched as first one and then another person "got it." Some people, like certain straight-laced contemporary readers of *A Modest Proposal,* never got the joke.

Because of the performance problem with anticontextual structures, I would guess that works of genre A emerged before works of genre B. Similarly, works of genre C before works of genre D. The field work to test the former hypothesis is still to be correlated. But the latter hypothesis seems to be born out, at least by the development of the English novel. However, whether genre C would emerge before or after genre B, or whether there could be any rule for this in light of other nonstructural factors that might affect the development of genres, is a question on which I am not willing to speculate.

The Mixing of Genres

Although I would not make assertions about the details of a literary history for a given literary community, I think it is fairly safe to make certain guesses about the practice of that community at any given time. Assuming that more than one generic possibility exists for artists of that community, I would guess that genres would mix with a frequency directly proportional to their structural similarity. That is, the closer together two genres are spatially in figure 4 (p. 158), the more frequent will be examples of works that mix those two genres. Let us briefly consider this hypothesis for modern English language narratives.

Genres E and F, as has been pointed out above, must to some extent assimilate structures from other narrative genres in order to maintain narrative voice. If this proposition about structural similarity is correct, we would assume that comedy most frequently assimilates the structure of romance; tragedy the structure of the realistic novel. This seems to me true in a case such as Austen, where we have the inevitable marriage we expect in so many romances of the *Daphnis and Chloe* type; or in a case such as *An American Tragedy,* which depends so much on the structure of a realistic novel. But we should be able to expand this principle, and see romance appropriating epic and folk tale, realistic novels appropriating the picaresque and the satire. This, of course, we can find, when the romance is Chaucer's "Knight's Tale"; or when the realistic fiction is American Southwestern humor, like *Huckleberry Finn.*

In addition to this, I would guess that, second only to the ease of appropriating structural possibilities from adjoining genres in the same *column,* would be the ease of appropriating structural possibilities from the adjoining genre in the same *rank.* That is, romance would most easily assimilate structures from genre A or genre E, but after these one would expect the assimilation of genre D. It does seem that reversing the principle of contextuality would be more fundamental and therefore more difficult than multiplying or simplifiying contexts. For this reason I would speculate that the number of C/A (predominantly romance, but appropriating structures of genre A, folk tale to epic) works or C/E works would greatly outnumber C/D works. However, by multiplying the difficulty of assimilation, we can guess quite logically that the number of C/D works outnumbers the C/B works; they are related diagonally in figure 4. That is, romance will more commonly appropriate realistic structures than satiric structures. Such a hypothesis, if it proved to be justified, would indicate that the generic grid not only maps out possibilities for the use of suspense, but indicates the distribution of the combinations of these possibilities.

I would like to suggest here a notation. In order to test this hypothesis, and also for general descriptive purposes, we would want some way of easily noting the diachronic structure we discover in a given work. I suggest that the formulaic expression for narrative structure follow this paradigm: $x/y(z)$, where x stands for the dominant structure, y stands for the assimilated structure, and z records the level(s) at which that structure is assimilated. For example, in this formulation, we would describe the structure of the *Odyssey* as A/C (plot); the structure of *Bleak House* as E/F(style). Using such a notation, it should be relatively easy to gather the data needed to determine the value of the generic grid in predicting the frequency of occurrence of structural possibilities in narrative.

Modal Possibilities

The notation we now have allows us to express compactly the gross diachronic structure of a narrative. Since this is a diachronic notation, each of its terms will imply something about the functioning of suspense. It is for this reason that the notation made no provision for incorporating information about the side of the range (emphasis on individual or on society) within a genre toward which a given work might fall. That is, "The Ghost Wife" and the *Aeneid* would both be described as A/O, genre A with no assimilation.

However, anyone making *in*clusive genre distinctions would want to note a multitude of differences between these works. The point to bear in mind here is that these are not structural differences. On the other hand, this study has not yet considered two important camps in literature: allegoric narrative and parodic narrative: *The Faerie Queene* would be an example of the former, *Joseph Andrews* an example of the latter. I would like to advance yet another hypothesis.

In a work like *Joseph Andrews*, we have two important phenomena, a romance like *Pamela*, and something that seems to play with that romance in order to undercut it. In a sense, we have five levels of narration: the four of the romance, and a fifth stylistic level which stands in some relation to the whole of the other integrated four. To borrow the conclusions of Boris Eichenbaum, and to distinguish this from the structure of *satire*, I would call a work that had these five levels and in which the fifth undercut the other four *parody*. Of parody, Eichenbaum says

> . . . as a stylistic device [it is] one of the manifestations (having great historical-literary significance) of the dialectical development of literary groups.[5]

In the same way that bits can compare anti-contextually, the fifth level in *Joseph Andrews* compares *antigenerically* with the other four. The introduction of antigeneric comparison seems to me a step in the development from (or the mixing of) romance and realistic novel.

The particular structure, then, which is parody, seems to me to modulate our engagement with a text. For that reason, I would like to call parody a *modal* possibility; parody becomes overt only when there is a sufficiently ramified and coherent structure against which the fifth stylistic level can compare antigenerically. If one is further willing to speculate that the coherent structure need not be built through literary allusion, but can be built through image-structures that relate to social organization (social parody), or even philosophic arguments (logical parody), then the exact modal hypothesis would be the following two-part theorem: (1) There are three modal possibilities which are analogous to the three possibilities of contextuality: antigeneric modality (parody; *Joseph Andrews*), neutral modality (in which, like the works we have considered, a four-level structural analysis is sufficient to describe the working of suspense), and progeneric modality (allegory; *Faerie Queene*); (2) The basic engagement of suspense with a text depends upon the primary genre, and simultaneously the enveloping mode. This means that if we take a four-level analysis of the *Faerie Queene* to result in a description such as A/C(plot) (epic, but assimilating romance at the level of plot), then we should say that suspense functions here in just this way (A/C(plot)), but at any point in the reading there is a further diachronic structure which produces a progeneric comparison of the underlying structure with another coherent structure (Christianity). We could say then, if such an hypothesis proved to be true, that we should be able to find examples of both parody and allegory in any of our genres, and that the engagement we feel with such works is similar to the engagement with any works of those genres, but complicated by the modality. To expand the notation, we would express the structure of the *Odyssey* as A/C(plot), but of the *Faerie Queene* as A(+)/C(plot); *Joseph Andrews,* assuming that *Pamela's* structure is C/O, would be C(−)/O. Since we no more notice modality in the neutral case than we notice rhetoric in the neutral case, we need not mark that mode. Thus, + would stand for an allegoric modality (a metaphoric relation of the fifth stylistic level to the other integrated four), − for a parodic modality (an ironic relationship of the fifth level to the other four), and we would not mark neutrally modulated works.

The hypothesis that the engagement with a modulated work depends upon the primary genre which is modulated seems to me to facilitate discussion of a number of critical problems. How, for example, shall one discuss the relationship between the *Faerie Queene* and *Pilgrim's Progress?* The position behind this hypothesis leads to the following analytic procedure: identify the primary genres of each work (say A/C(plot) for *Faerie Queene,* and A/O for *Pilgrim's Progress*), identify the modality of each work (+ in each case, allegory), and then make relevant comparisons among the details of these results (e.g., study the effect of having a more complicated plot; compare the coherent positions in the fifth levels).

The results of studies carried out in light of this hypothesis, I would speculate, would have three important effects: (1) they would supply more exact data for the kind of literary history suggested above; (2) they would give greater structural detail for the discussion of the mixing of genres; (3) they would remind us that modality is always, even in the neutral and therefore undramatic case, a concern in studying the structure of a narrative.[6]

A Moving Aesthetic

Finally, I would like to speculate on the problem of aesthetic prescription, the possibility of articulating rules for art. In order to test one's principles, one must always make an analysis that does not depend upon those principles. A failure to follow this logical theorem results in circular reasoning. Returning to our house-hunting couple, one may ask about the quality of construction of a building. If our couple assumes that frame construction and brass plumbing indicate good construction, then they are fully equipped to find a house which has frame construction and brass plumbing. But they are only equipped to find a well-constructed home if their assumptions have been correct. The only way to test those assumptions is to have criteria that do not depend on them. That is, if a criterion for good construction is durability, then they may find that frame construction and brass plumbing never need repair, and *therefore* can be used as principles for discovering a well-built home. Similarly, if we wish to test aesthetic formulations (e.g., variety, unity or coherence),[7] the one means by which we can*not* analyze works of art is that means which depends on the aesthetic formulation in question. Structural analysis presents an alternative means.

I would guess that an investigation using the kind of structural tools here developed would corroborate the value of at least two of the three most common aesthetic formulations. The position that narrative art depends upon suspense would seem to indicate that there must first be something, and then something else. Question-and-answer is the type of this structure; one could look upon it as a principle of variety. And something like unity or coherence, we may speculate, would also be implied.

I would like to couch this last formulation in terms more appropriate to the methods this study has developed. In any of the extended narratives which have been discussed in part only, I have induced that the analysis would hold for the whole. The Souvarine paragraph from *Germinal,* for example (p. 138), strikes me as *typical* of the whole narrative. It feels the same to read that paragraph, that is, subliminal suspense operates in it, exactly as in the entire book. In light of this, I would advance the following aesthetic dictum: if one studies a sufficiently large portion (often merely a sentence) of a narrative to elucidate the diachronic structure of the whole, no part of that whole should deviate from the structure so determined. Such a formulation is semantically equivalent to some notion of either coherence or unity, but I believe that stated this way it helps remind the critic that his material is the *experience* of reading. Such an aesthetic dictum is based on a willingness to accept the importance of suspense structures. However, this willingness is motivated not only by practical criticism, but by the empirical conclusions of nonliterary disciplines. That is, this formulation makes aesthetics emphasize the way *form feels,* and this, I think, is how readers respond.[8]

Title

For a writer in the throes of a book, and for a reader when he has finished with it, the title should serve somehow to recall the heart of the matter. "When Slim turned sideways . . ." has done this for me as writer, and I would like to explain its importance for me in the hope that it may then serve equally for the reader. "When Slim turned sideways . . ." is the first half of a line, as I remember it, from *Pecos Bill,* a book that I read when I was twelve. Twelve, it seems to me, is a good time to catch a reader if we want to ask him questions about the way a book works. At that age, it is clear that people read through some compulsion that is worked by the book. But as we become older, or more learned, or both, we get used to language, and we only notice its power when it deviates from the norm, or, in this case, when half a line is withheld. There is suspense in such a half line, metaphor in the name, questions of action and character to be answered. All of these things are what make the suspense that is at the heart of a good book. But they vanish when our concern shifts to questions asked after the reading is done, when the experience has become a motionless memory. I have tried to remind myself of those things in this book, for after the book is done, and when I go back into the reading of another story, these questions will become again subliminal. But that is what makes them so important. "When Slim turned sideways, his shadow disappeared."

Notes

INTRODUCTION

1. Gaston Bachelard, *The Poetics of Space* (Boston: Beacon Press; 1969), p. 9.
2. T. S. Eliot, cited in Rene Wellek and Austin Warren, *Theory of Literature* (New York: Harvest Books, 1956), p. 241.
3. Edward Taylor, "The Preface," in *The American Tradition in Literature*, Bradley, Beatty, Long, eds., vol. 1 (New York: W. W. Norton & Co., 1962), p. 64.
4. Janie Tarlow, *Sex Sorceress* (New York: Spade Publishing, Inc., 1969).
5. See the works of Karl Mannheim.
6. This, of course, relates directly to Coleridge's famous "willing suspension of disbelief."
7. Herman Melville, *Typee* (New York: Signet Classic, 1964).
8. Marshall McLuhan, *Understanding Media: The Extensions of Man* (New York: McGraw-Hill Paperbacks, 1966).

CHAPTER I

1. Michael Polanyi, *The Tacit Dimension* (New York: Doubleday Anchor Books, 1967), p. 4.
2. E. H. Gombrich, *Art and Illusion* (Princeton: Bollingen Series, 1969), chap. 7.
3. Polanyi, op. cit.
4. Will Rogers, *The Illiterate Digest* (New York: Albert and Charles Boni, 1924), pp. 269-70.

5. We doubt the interest of an author in his own materials as a last resort. Normally, because the materials have been put into a narrative frame by the author, and come to us in that frame, we assume they are fit objects of interest. The whole function of the frame is to partition that which is to be focused on from that which is not. It is our subliminal acceptance of this notion of frames that Andy Warhol plays on with his Campbell soup cans.

6. I. A. Richards, *Practical Criticism* (New York: Harvest Books, 1956), p. 6.

7. Ibid., p. 7.

8. Our normal inability to notice that which functions subliminally until something later in the text calls it to our attention serves in large measure to validate the New Critical dictum that we must read and reread a poem before we begin the process of criticism. See I. A. Richards, *Practical Criticism.*

9. Oscar Wilde, cited in William K. Wimsatt, Jr., and Cleanth Brooks, *Literary Criticism: A Short History* (New York: Vintage Books, 1957), p. 748.

10. Northrop Frye, Philip Wheelwright, et al.

11. Wimsatt and Brooks, op. cit., chap. 32.

12. This nomenclature is used as I. A. Richards develops it in *The Philosophy of Rhetoric,* chaps. 5 and 6.

13. William Dean Howells, *A Modern Instance* (New York: Signet Classic, 1964), p. 153.

14. I have chosen a "dead" metaphor here because it more easily reveals its structure than a "live" one. However, as Richards has pointed out, "dead metaphor" is itself a metaphor, and no metaphor is so dead that a poet cannot rouse it to life.

15. Albert Payson Terhune, *Gray Dawn* (New York: Harper & Brothers Publishers, 1927), p. 1.

16. We could use these terms by extending them, as Richards sometimes seems to imply we should; however, they would still preserve an erroneous two-part notion of metaphor: "If we cannot distinguish tenor from vehicle then we may provisionally take the word to be literal; if we can distinguish at least two co-operating uses, then we have metaphor." I. A. Richards, *The Philosophy of Rhetoric* (New York: Oxford University Press, 1965), p. 119.

17. Indeed, if Frank Kermode is correct in *The Sense of an Ending* (New York: Oxford University Press, 1968), the notion of

looking forward for formal completion underlies not only our reading, but all aspects of our thinking as well.

18. James Agee, *A Death in the Family* (New York: Avon Books, 1966), p. 35.
19. Joseph Heller, *Catch-22* (New York: Dell Books, 1967), p. 169.
20. *Recontextualizing* is borrowed from Philip Wheelwright. "A poet's way with symbols is by recontextualizing to give them new life." *Metaphor and Reality* (Bloomington, Ind.: Midland Books, 1968), p. 96.
21. Herman Melville, *Moby-Dick* (New York: Bobbs-Merrill Co., Inc., 1964), p. 148.
22. It is, of course, significant that these are all romances.
23. Ernest Hemingway, *The Sun Also Rises* (New York: Charles Scribner's Sons, 1954), p. 11.
24. Dreiser worked quite carefully from newspaper accounts of a much reported drowning and the subsequent trial of the murderer.
25. J. Morton, "A Preliminary Functional Model for Language Behaviour," in *Language,* R. C. Oldfield and J. C. Marshall, eds. (Baltimore: Penguin Books, 1968), pp. 152-53.
26. A. R. Luria, "The Directive Function of Speech in Development and Dissolution, Part I," in Oldfield and Marshall, op. cit., p. 73.
27. Anton Chekov, "Gooseberries," in Anton Tchekoff, *The House with the Mezzanine and other stories,* trans. S. S. Koteliansky and Gilbert Cannan (New York: Charles Scribner's Sons, 1917).
28. J. Morton, op. cit.
29. Nathaniel Hawthorne, "The Great Carbuncle," in *The Complete Novels and Selected Tales of Nathaniel Hawthorne,* Norman Holmes Pearson, ed. (New York: Modern Library, 1937), pp. 927-37.
30. E. M. Forster, *Aspects of the Novel* (New York: Harvest Books, 1954), pp. 31-32.
31. Lionel Trilling, "Freud and Literature," in *Criticism: The Foundations of Modern Literary Judgment,* Mark Schorer, Josephine Miles, and Gordon McKenzie, eds. (New York: Harcourt, Brace and Company, 1958), p. 181.
32. Bachelard, op. cit., p. 17.
33. Norman N. Holland, *The Dynamics of Literary Response* (New York: Oxford University Press, 1968).

34. See Erik H. Erikson, *Childhood and Society* (New York: W. W. Norton, 1963).
35. R. Brown, "How Shall a Thing be Called?" in Oldfield and Marshall, op. cit.
36. Ibid., pp. 90-91.
37. Henry James, *The Wings of the Dove* (New York: Dell Books, 1953), p. 19.
38. This may be due, in part, to the dehumanizing of individuals that McLuhan attributes to the medium of the daily newspaper.
39. Here, as elsewhere, I must acknowledge my indebtedness to Larry W. Martin's incisive presentation and treatment of the problems of linguistics.
40. Susanne K. Langer, *An Introduction to Symbolic Logic* (New York: Dover, 1953), esp. chaps. 2 and 7.
41. J. R. R. Tolkien, *The Hobbit* (New York: Ballantine Books, 1965), p. 15.
42. William Empson, *7 Types of Ambiguity* (New York: New Directions, n.d.).
43. Thomas Wolfe, *Look Homeward, Angel* (New York: Charles Scribner's Sons, 1952), pp. 404-5.
44. Empson, op. cit., p. 1.
45. Thomas Dekker, *Selected Prose Writings,* E. D. Pendry, ed. (Cambridge, Mass.: Harvard University Press, 1968), p. 182.
46. Maurice Merleau-Ponty, *The Primacy of Perception and Other Essays,* James M. Edie, ed. (Evanston, Ill.: Northwestern University Press, 1964).
47. Bachelard, op. cit., and *The Psychoanalysis of Fire* (Boston: Beacon Press, 1968).
48. From William Faulkner, *As I Lay Dying* (New York: Vintage Books, 1957).
49. Henry James, "The Turn of the Screw," in Henry James, *The Turn of the Screw and Other Short Novels* (New York: Signet Classic, 1962), p. 291.
50. There is also here a latent phenomenological structure (built on *Christmas, child,* and *visitation*) that predicts the possibility of salvation. This possibility stands against the ghost story motifs to create a tension which is quite important to the story as a whole.
51. Bachelard, *The Poetics of Space,* op. cit., p. 72.
52. Gustav Flaubert, *Sentimental Education* (New York: Everyman's Library, 1961), p. 27.

53. Laurence Sterne, *Tristram Shandy* (New York: Everyman's Library, 1964), p. 3.
54. Sterne's periodic sentences are not, obviously, as mechanically perfect as, say, Burke's. The embedded clauses are not isocolons. One may wish to treat their deviation from the rhetoric book model as itself another example of anticontextuality.
55. William Faulkner, *Absalom, Absalom!* (New York: Modern Library Book, 1964), p. 7.
56. Jane Austen, *Pride and Prejudice* (Boston: Riverside Editions, 1956), p. 1.
57. See Mark Schorer's introduction to Austen, op. cit., p. xi.
58. Such a view is practically inescapable since Wayne Booth published *The Rhetoric of Fiction* (Chicago: University of Chicago Press, 1968).
59. *The Random House Dictionary of the English Language* (New York, 1966), p. 1433.
60. M. H. Abrams, *A Glossary of Literary Terms* (New York: Holt, Rinehart & Winston, 1962), p. 70.
61. Edgar Allan Poe, "Narrative of A. Gordon Pym," in *The Complete Tales and Poems of Edgar Allan Poe* (New York: Modern Library, 1938).
62. James D. Hart, *The Oxford Companion to American Literature* (New York: Oxford University Press, 1965), pp. 452-53.
63. Nathanael West, *Miss Lonelyhearts,* in *Miss Lonelyhearts & The Day of the Locust* (New York: New Directions Paperback, 1962).

CHAPTER II

1. Charles Feidelson, Jr., *Symbolism and American Literature* (Chicago: University of Chicago Press, 1966), p. 169.
2. See John T. Frederick, *The Darkened Sky* (Notre Dame, Ind.: University of Notre Dame Press, 1969).
3. Nathaniel Hawthorne, *The Marble Faun,* in Nathaniel Hawthorne, op. cit.
4. Henry James, cited in Wimsatt and Brooks, op. cit., p. 37.
5. Forster, op. cit., p. 6.
6. Northrop Frye, *The Anatomy of Criticism* (New York: Atheneum Publishers, 1968), pp. 158-243.
7. Mark Twain, "The Man That Corrupted Hadleyburg," Bradley, Beatty, and Long, op. cit., vol. 2, pp. 220-21.

8. Isak Dinesen, "Of The Millennium," in *The World's Shortest Stories*, Richard G. Hubler, ed. (New York: Duell, Sloan & Pearce, 1961), p. 171.
9. Martial, "On Galla," in Hubler, op. cit., p. 135.
10. Anton Chekov, "Vanka," in Hubler, op. cit., pp. 4-7.
11. Arthur Koestler, *Insight and Outlook* (Lincoln: University of Nebraska Press, 1949).
12. See Erich Auerbach, *Mimesis* (Princeton: Princeton University Press, 1968), chaps. 5 and 6.
13. The best explication of the latent content of a particular joke is probably the first chapter of Norman Holland's *The Dynamics of Literary Response* (New York: Oxford University Press, 1968).

CHAPTER III

1. Vladimir Propp, *The Morphology of the Folktale* (Austin: University of Texas Press, 1968).
2. See Claude Lévi-Strauss, *Structural Anthropology* (Garden City, N.Y.: Anchor Books, 1967), chap. 11.
3. George Bird Grinnell, *Pawnee Hero Stories and Folk-tales* (Lincoln: University of Nebraska Press, 1961), pp. 129-31.
4. See Ruth Benedict, *Patterns of Culture* (New York: Mentor Books, 1959), chap. 4.
5. Frye, op. cit., pp. 315-26.
6. Albert B. Lord, *The Singer of Tales* (New York: Atheneum Publishers, 1968).
7. A good summary of Lord's position is available in Robert Scholes and Robert Kellogg, *The Nature of Narrative* (New York: Oxford University Press, 1966), chap. 2.
8. Lord, op. cit., p. 68.
9. Lillian Herland Hornstein, et al., *The Reader's Companion to World Literature* (New York: Mentor Books, 1956), p. 10.
10. Homer is slightly more complex structurally than Vergil. This difference is discussed later in the text.
11. Vergil, *The Works of Vergil*, John Dryden, trans. (London: Oxford University Press, 1961), p. 131.
12. Hornstein, et al., op. cit., p. 9.
13. "Lazarillo de Tormes," in *Masterpieces of the Spanish Golden Age*, Angel Flores, ed. (New York: Holt, Rinehart and Winston, 1963), p. 74.
14. *Friar* operates anticontextually as *master* also because of the vow of poverty that the clergy swore.

15. Hart, op. cit., p. 57.
16. I am indebted for this insight to Professor David Hayman.
17. See Sir Paul Harvey, *The Oxford Companion to English Literature* (Oxford: Oxford University Press, 1967), p. 282.
18. *Howleglas,* in *A Hundred Merry Tales,* P. M. Zall, ed. (Lincoln: University of Nebraska Press, 1963), pp. 176-77.
19. Ibid., introduction.
20. See note 22.
21. Jonathan Swift, *Gulliver's Travels and Other Writings* (Boston: Riverside Editions, 1960), pp. 44-45.
22. This may be apparently complicated by a confusion between satire as a structure and traditional satire which sometimes includes other structures. See the section on modal possibilities below for an attempt to clarify this confusion.
23. Longus, *Daphnis and Chloe* (Baltimore: Penguin Classics, 1968).
24. The subordination here of the surface anticontextuality to a procontextual principle of which we are subliminally aware is analogous to the alternating recontextualizations in Melville (see p. 20). There the controlling context is the narrative voice. Melville's works, of course, are usually considered to be romantic.
25. Gottfried von Strassburg, *Tristan* (Baltimore: Penguin Classics, 1960).
26. Hawthorne, Preface to *Blithedale Romance,* in Hawthorne, op. cit., p. 439.
27. See Wolfgang Köhler, *Gestalt Psychology* (New York: Mentor Books, 1961), for a good introduction.
28. See Florence Kluckhohn and F. Strodtbeck, *Variations in Value Orientation* (Evanston, Ill.: Roe, Peterson, 1961), for a good introduction.
29. Koestler, op. cit., p. 37.
30. Frank Kermode, *The Sense of an Ending,* op. cit.
31. T. E. Hulme, *Speculations,* Herbert Read, ed. (New York: Harvest Books, 1924).
32. See Lee T. Lemon and Marion J. Reis, trans. and eds., *Russian Formalist Criticism Four Essays* (Lincoln: University of Nebraska Press, Bison Books, 1965).
33. Victor Shklovsky, "Art as Technique," in Lemon and Reis, op. cit., p. 12.
34. William Dean Howells, *A Modern Instance* (New York: Signet Classic, 1964).

35. Henry James, *The Ambassadors* (Boston: Riverside Editions, 1960), p. 365.
36. Emile Zola, *Germinal* (Baltimore: Penguin Classics, 1968).
37. See Wayne Booth, *The Rhetoric of Fiction*, op. cit.
38. See Frye, op. cit., passim.
39. Charles Dickens, *Bleak House* (Boston: Riverside Editions, 1956).
40. Edwin Muir, *The Structure of the Novel* (London: Hogarth Press, 1967).
41. Boris Tomashevsky, "Thematics," in Lemon and Reis, op. cit., p. 89.
42. Jane Austen, *Emma* (Boston: Riverside Editions, 1957), p. 381.
43. See how Tomashevsky, op. cit., treats the relationship between a narrative's protagonist and its arrangement of motifs.
44. Dickens, *Hard Times* (New York: Rinehart Editions, 1965).
45. Dickens, *David Copperfield* (New York: Books Inc., 1868).
46. See Victor Shklovsky, "Sterne's *Tristram Shandy:* Stylistic Commentary," in Lemon and Reis, op. cit., pp. 25-59, for a complete analysis.
47. Tom Lehrer, "Oedipus Rex," on the album *More of Tom Lehrer* (Cambridge, Mass.: Lehrer Records/TL102, 1959).
48. Holland, op. cit., pp. 3-4.
49. Thomas Mann, *Death in Venice and Seven Other Stories* (New York: Vintage Books, 1936), p. 3.

CHAPTER IV

1. See Walter Goldschmidt, "The Ethical Prescriptions of Yurok Society," in *Exploring the Ways of Mankind,* Walter Goldschmidt, ed. (New York: Holt, Rinehart and Winston, 1966), pp. 544-54.
2. See Robert Ardrey, *African Genesis* (New York: Dell, 1967), esp. chap. 2.
3. For this distinction, and much of what follows from it, I am indebted to conversations with Larry W. Martin at the University of Iowa, 1969-70.
4. This has been the repeated observation of my wife in her career as an elementary school teacher.

5. Boris Eichenbaum, "The Theory of the 'Formal Method'," in Lemon and Reis, op. cit., p. 134.

6. A detailed study of the problem of mode should be available in Professor David Hayman's forthcoming book. Here, as elsewhere, I must acknowledge my personal and intellectual debt to a good friend and stimulating teacher.

7. Professor Robert Scholes has pointed out to me the pervasive use of these criteria in aesthetic studies.

8. If this last speculation is true, that a part of a narrative should in some basic and subliminal way be representative of the feeling of reading the whole, then we can draw one very important pedagogic implication: it is possible for us as teachers to say much of what is important about reading a book on the basis of an analysis of its first pages, or a single representative section.

It has been my experience, which I trust I share with most teachers of literature, that students do not come into the classroom having finished a work. If one assigns, on a Friday, the reading of *Moby Dick* for Monday, one is fortunate if every student in the class has read the first two hundred pages. One may find that not a single student has finished the book, and some have not begun it. But an analysis of "The Lee Shore" put in terms of the details of temporally extended linguistic effects would clearly add to the students' reading not only of that chapter, but of the entire work. And most of the class will have read as far as page 148. If they haven't, they can still read along.

I am not suggesting here that, once a class has some control of the work as a whole, biographical criticism, historical criticism, or allusive criticism is not both useful and important. Certainly no literary scholar should read *Moby Dick* without considering the success of *Typee,* Manifest Destiny, or the frequent Biblical references. But our students do not come to us as scholars, although we hope that some of them may leave that way. Nor do we approach a new book as scholars. We are readers foremost. New Criticism, especially as I. A. Richards exemplifies it in *Practical Criticism,* is both a pedagogic tactic and a critical method. As a critical method, it yields much fruit. But as a tactic, I think it fails to consider the student, the average student, who does not walk into the room on that first day of discussion having all the parts of a work firmly in mind, ready to be compared, considered, rearranged, and discussed. New Criticism is not sufficient for the teaching of reading. And the problem that we must always confront in literature is the problem of reading. I offer diachronic analysis as a pedagogic solution.

Glossary

The following terms are glossed because the author recognizes that they may be unfamiliar, or used in nonstandard ways. This listing is intended to remind the reader after he has put the book away of those special concepts which might be of use to him.

bisociation: drawn from Koestler's *Insight and Outlook,* this term as used here is intended to refer to the process by which, or the instant at which, two contexts come to be involved meaningfully at a single moment of reading, e.g., in the punchline of a joke.

bit: as in computer technology, a bit is a unit which has meaning in isolation, but which, it is assumed, will take on other meanings, or enter into other meanings, when used in special relations with other bits or in various contexts. In this sense, a reader could equally well perceive, even though subliminally, a bit of stylistic information as a bit of plot information.

comparison: early in the discussion, comparison is the general case of a perceived bit in relation to its relevant eidetic bit or the context which that eidetic bit has revivified. More exactly, we reserve *comparison* to refer to the relation of a *single* perceived bit to a *single* eidetic bit, or to a *single* context.

context: the total mental freight which a reader must carry forward in order to integrate the significance of a perceived bit into his total reading of a narrative.

contextuality: the general term for the relationship that holds between the perceived bit and either the eidetic bit or the context. When the perceived bit supports the context, the relationship (bisociation or comparison) is procontextual; when it undercuts the context, the relationship is anticontextual; when there is no apparent redefinition of the bit due to the context, the relationship is neutral. (At the level of style, these varieties of contextuality are, respectively, metaphor, irony, and propositional statement.)

diachronic: extended in temporal sequence; when used of narrative structure, diachronic denotes that structure which follows the order of perception of bits in time as one normally reads or listens.

discharge: that type of comparison or bisociation in which the result seems to have no continuing, implicit diachronic structure. Although we may be left with an ironic truth at the end of a joke, the punchline clearly ends the narrative structure: the bisociating contexts discharge each other.

genre: in logic, any class; here, classes of narratives. The theoretical genres which are schematized on p. 158 are derived by permuting theoretical distinctions. The overlap of these theoretical genres with the traditional genres which have been classed intuitively merely indicates that both the theory and the intuitions are closely concerned with the affect of the reading process.

image-structure: the structural relations implied by the uses of images. These may be of three kinds: *functional,* to call a metal disk a dime indicates that it functions in its narrative world as a monetary denomination rather than a physical object; *phenomenal,* certain phenomena seem to characteristically organize certain emotions or attitudes, e.g., time and the river; *nexal,* some images ordinarily predict future states, e.g., the "thunderhead effect."

interest: used to denote the engagement that any individual reader may feel with any part of a text regardless of the diachronic structure of the text, e.g., Marxist critics are interested in books about revolution.

levels of narration: the arbitrary divisions of the integrated narrative into strands which persist diachronically throughout. These divisions are style, plot, theme, and character, each considered in a developmental way. Such arbitrary division must be ultimately recognized as inappropriate to the whole text, though useful for study.

modality: the general term for the relationship that holds between an integrated allusive structure (set off as a fifth level of narration, a second stylistic level) and the other integrated four levels of the primary narrative. This relationship can be of three kinds: the fifth level can support the other four (progeneric; allegory); the fifth level can undercut the other four (antigeneric; parody); or the fifth level may not appear as rhetorically separate from the other four (neutral; primary genres).

Glossary

plot: as in the Formalists, the order of events as presented. The structure of plot gives rise to the common perception of plot suspense, a variety of the general notion of suspense.

residue: that which remains after a comparison or bisociation, and implies a continuing diachronic structure.

structure: unless stated otherwise, always intended in this study to refer to diachronic structure. Such structures may be of two types: image- and syntax-structures.

subliminal suspense: that engagement with structure which involves us in waiting for formal completion but of which we are not consciously aware.

suspense: the general term for the engagement with structure. It is in this sense reasonable to speak of plot-suspense when considering plot-structure, style-suspense when considering style-structure, and so forth. Further, we can distinguish between the unconscious subliminal-suspense and the conscious varieties which may be either potential (not directly necessary for completing the structure of the level in which they arise) or necessary.

synchronic: existing at the same time, or out of time. This concept is useful in studying myths.

syntax-structure: the unconscious structure implied by the very nature of the language; a diachronic structure of which we are never consciously aware unless it is somehow interfered with, as in the case of . . .

voice: an anthropomorphized notion of the continuing presence that keeps us within the narrative world and ameliorates the completeness of any discharges except the last.

186

Selected Bibliography

Bachelard, Gaston. *The Poetics of Space.* Boston: Beacon Press, 1969.

———.*The Psychoanalysis of Fire.* Boston: Beacon Press, 1968.

Barthes, Roland. *Writing Degree Zero.* New York: Hill and Wang, 1968.

Forster, E. M. *Aspects of the Novel.* New York: Harvest Books, 1954.

Gombrich, E. H. *Art and Illusion.* Princeton: Bollingen Series, Princeton University Press, 1969.

Holland, Norman N. *The Dynamics of Literary Response.* New York: Oxford University Press, 1968.

Kermode, Frank. *The Sense of an Ending.* New York: Oxford University Press, 1968).

Koestler, Arthur. *Insight and Outlook.* Lincoln: University of Nebraska Press, 1949.

Köhler, Wolfgang. *Gestalt Psychology.* New York: Mentor, 1961.

Lemon, Lee T., and Reis, Marion J., eds. *Russian Formalist Criticism: Four Essays.* Lincoln: University of Nebraska Press, 1965.

Lévi-Strauss, Claude. *Structural Anthropology.* New York: Anchor Books, 1967.

Lord, Albert B. *The Singer of Tales.* New York: Atheneum, 1968.

Merleau-Ponty, Maurice. *The Primacy of Perception and other essays.* Edited by James M. Edie. Evanston: Northwestern University Press, 1964.

Selected Bibliography

Oldfield, R. C., and Marshall, J. C., eds. *Language.* Baltimore: Penguin Classics, 1968.

Polanyi, Michael. *The Tacit Dimension.* New York: Doubleday Anchor Books, 1967.

Propp, Vladimir. *Morphology of the Folktale.* Austin: University of Texas Press, 1968.

Richards, I. A. *The Philosophy of Rhetoric.* New York: Oxford University Press, 1965.

———. *Practical Criticism.* New York: Harvest Books, 1929.

Scholes, Robert, and Kellogg, Robert. *The Nature of Narrative.* New York: Oxford University Press, 1968.

Wheelwright, Philip. *Metaphor and Reality.* Bloomington: Indiana University Press, 1968.

Index

Index

Index